OVERCOMING MEDIOCRITY

To Susan,

Love,

Deanna

INFLUENTIAL WOMEN

OVERCOMING *Mediocrity* ©

A unique collection of stories from influential women who have created their own lives of significance!

Presented by Christie L. Ruffino

DPWN Publishing

www.overcomingmediocrity.org

For more information, contact:
DPWN Publishing
A division of the Dynamic Professional Women's Network, Inc.
1879 N. Neltnor Blvd. #316, West Chicago, IL 60185
www.overcomingmediocrity.org
www.ourdpwn.com

Printed in the United States of America

ISBN: 978-1-939794-12-3

Dedication

To every woman who does not believe she can make a difference and to every woman who believes she can move a mountain.

To every woman who continually makes sacrifices for those she loves and to every woman who prioritizes those moments when she can pamper and take care of her own needs.

To every woman who believes that she should settle for the life she has and to every woman who has overcome great odds to create her own life of significance.

To the resilient women in this book who have shared their stories with you in hopes that their lessons of pain will become your lessons of power.

To the women in my life who believe I am significant and whom I believe are priceless.

The Power of Our Story

There is nothing more important in this world than the relationships we build and the legacy we leave in the lives of those who have crossed paths with us on our journey of life. It's the experiences we have along this journey that define our individual uniqueness and creates our own powerful personal blueprint or our unique story snowflake.

It is this blueprint that can empower us to possess a distinct advantage over every other person in this world if leveraged correctly and shared. If we don't have the courage to share our snowflake, it will be lost forever. No one will have the same story and no one can repeat your story. Therefore, those who come after you will never learn anything from what you experienced and what you learned.

I feel that the most significant thing we can do to add value back into this world is to master the narrative of our lives. All of our leadership and moneymaking abilities rest in our ability to discover, craft and deliver our personal story or message in a way that will allow people to connect to us. The right story shared at the right time with the right person can alter the trajectory of their life.

We also have the ability to learn from other people's stories and change the direction of the stories we are living to shape our ultimate destinies.

Power to you and the story of your life!

Know that wherever you are in your life right now is both temporary, and exactly where you are supposed to be. You have arrived at this moment to learn what you must learn, so you can become the person you need to be to create the life you truly want. Even when life is difficult or challenging—especially when life is difficult and challenging—the present is always an opportunity for us to learn, grow, and become better than we've ever been before.

— Hal Elrod

Introduction

Welcome to our sixth *Overcoming Mediocrity* book featuring an amazing lineup of influential women. The stories in this book are about strength, faith, and courage. They are about having the confidence to believe in ourselves, even when those we love don't. They are about having the courage to do things that are hard, even when we may not want to. And they are about remaining resilient through all of life's ups and downs because that is what, as women, we do brilliantly.

Our first *Overcoming Mediocrity* book was a smashing success! It was released in 2013 with 22 women sharing their stories to inspire other women to overcome and succeed as they did. That book became the #1 downloaded Kindle book in the motivational genre category on the very first day of its release, allowing the authors to claim the distinguished Amazon Bestselling Author status. It was so exciting!

My initial goal with this project was to create one collaborative book, collecting incredible stories from women I admired who were friends and members of the Dynamic Professional Women's Network (DPWN). I knew how transformational an experience like this had been for me when I was asked to share my story in a similar book compiled by a mentor of mine, Michelle Prince. I also knew how having a book to share in the business community gave me additional credibility and exposure. What I didn't know was how transformational the stories would be for the readers who related with one or more of the women inside that first book. Those blessings would come later.

I had built a thriving membership organization providing women a successful system to build a strong referral network as a DPWN member, so it was a logical transition to also provide them an opportunity to share their stories like I did. This would allow them the opportunity to leverage "Author" status and gain additional exposure and credibility for their business. It would also enable them to receive greater blessings as they collaborated with other authors and shared their stories with a wider audience. These books have ultimately taken on a life of their own and have made a greater impact than ever anticipated. It is exciting to read testimonials from women who have read one of the books and connected with the inspirational stories inside. It is even more exciting when one of those same women decide to share their story in one of our future books.

Because of the overwhelming success of that first book, we've gone on to produce additional books under the *Overcoming Mediocrity* brand. Each of them has also climbed to the #1 position on Amazon on the very first day. With our most recent book, *Overcoming Mediocrity—Resilient Women,* surprising us by reaching #1 in two categories.

And now, it is with great honor and pride that I am able to share with you stories from the influential women on the following pages of this book. I have had the pleasure of getting to know each of these ladies and learn a little about the stories they're sharing with you. I'm deeply inspired by the courage they're exhibiting for sharing the personal details of their lives with the sole intention of allowing you, the reader, to learn from their experiences. It is easy to become complacent and live a mediocre life, but these women made a choice to live lives of significance and share them with you throughout the pages of this book. This demonstrates courage and strength, as well as humility and the heart of a true go-giver. These women all have even greater things yet to come. They are women you should know, learn from, and emulate.

This book is not only meant to encourage you, but to also awaken you to recognizing the true value of collaboration. The women in this book want to make the biggest impact on the world by sharing their stories in a book that would get massive exposure and attempt to transform as many lives as possible. They could have kept their stories private. That would have been the safest and easiest path for them. But they decided to step out of their comfort zone and share the narrative of their lives with you.

I am blessed to have the opportunity to share this book with you. I hope you feel as blessed to receive the value these women and their stories offer you.

Hugs & Blessings,

Christie

Table of Contents

Shannon Ferraby

Believing in Your Value

She stood over eighty feet tall in what appeared to be a place of honor on our front lawn. For almost fifty years this strong, powerful and beautiful willow tree provided an oasis of shade and a home for wildlife. She towered over the other plants and trees and no doubt was the one they looked up to.

Until one day it all came crashing down. Literally.

While my husband was mowing the lawn, I carried our two-year-old son in my arms. Suddenly, a deafening noise filled the air. With no time to process where the boom had come from, or to contemplate moving out of harm's way, a giant limb of that grand willow crashed down beside us!

As the ground shook, I shook with fear as well! Had we been standing even a foot to the left, we might no longer be standing at all. Not long after, we had that mighty willow cut down to the stump. Where once stood a glorious, beautiful and useful tree, now sat a bare, exposed and worthless piece of something leftover. Willow might have preferred to hide in the woods, be taken away in pieces with the rest of herself or be ground into the dirt and just be done with it all. Instead, she sat hurt, useless and unable to move. She imagined the other plants and trees laughing at her fallen state. She lost her confidence in her ability to provide anything of beauty or value to her world.

She stayed that way for a very long time.

I stayed that way. For a *very long time*.

For many years, life was good. I was like Willow. I had grown up and was standing tall! I was secure and at peace with my place in the "yard." Oh sure, sometimes the wind blew and the rains came. But overall? I was happy! I felt loved, needed, appreciated and valued.

Until one day it all came crashing down. Much the same as Willow, I was cut down to the stump.

The felling began as one massive branch was hacked off after another.

We moved out of state, leaving behind family, friends and so much that I held dear. *Crack!*

We relocated to join a ministry. Soon after, everything fell apart and we found ourselves without a job, income or a place to serve. *Crash!*

Lonely and unsettled, we poured ourselves into serving in our new church. My fast and loud New Jersey personality didn't go over well in this small-town congregation. In the end, the elders called a meeting to talk to my husband about "getting his wife in order." *Slam!*

Not valued or wanted for who I was, I sat alone, in silence, with nothing to contribute and unable to serve.

With so many branches knocked down, I wasn't feeling like that beautiful willow anymore. I lost my confidence and was questioning why we moved. I doubted our ability to know what God really wanted of us. I was discouraged, deflated and had given up on many plans, hopes and dreams. Only one remained.

I can't remember a time far enough back that my deepest desire wasn't to adopt a child. After seventeen years of my husband not wanting anything to do with adoption, he had a change of heart. "Lord, could this be the reason you had us move here?" I wondered excitedly. After a year of our foster son living with us, in only three short weeks we would sign the final documents. We would be his mommy and daddy! Our home would be his forever home! In my heart, he was already my son. This dream was coming true! *WHAM!* Until it wasn't.

He called me Mommy. He signed his school papers using our last name.

He loved me. He trusted me. Then, one day, he decided to confide in me. I stayed calm throughout the day-long, back and forth conversation, strewed with bits of his heartbreaking tale. It was his tragedy that he had never told another living soul. As he said the final words to complete his story and confession, I died inside. My arms, hands, legs and even my tongue went numb. I loved him so much! I was hurting for all that he confessed to and all that had happened to him. I knew without a doubt that nothing he shared was his fault. But my son had just disclosed a parent's worst nightmare. My body went into shock. I couldn't breathe. In desperate need of help, I called our social worker.

Within seven hours I was cut down to a stump when our son was taken from us.

We were told that he would be placed in a home for just the weekend, to give everyone time to think and plan. They promised to call with a meeting time and location to gather on Tuesday. Tuesday came and went and they never called. I contacted the agency to insist on a meeting. I could feel what was left of me, the stump, begin to rot, when they finally replied and said there was no point. There would be no meeting. He would no longer be allowed to live in our home or *any* home with *any* children. "It's for the best," they said. "It's to protect your children," they said. "He'll get the help he needs," they said. "We'll find him another home," they said.

I could no longer hear their words through my hyperventilating cries and hysterical pleading. "He's my son!"

"He didn't get to say goodbye!"

"My children, his brothers and sisters, didn't even know he was leaving!"

"You can't do this! You can't just rip him away from us!"

"He loves us! He trusted me! Please! This isn't fair to him! He didn't mean it!"

"It's not his fault! Please! Don't punish *him* for this!"

"There must be another way!"

"I forgive him. I love him."

"Please…"

Suffocated.

Now I *was* confident again. I was confident that I was a failure at everything I tried to do. I failed at trying to make new friends after we moved. I failed in the ministry and in the church. I failed my husband and our parents by not protecting our children well enough. I failed my biological children and my son-to-be. Instead of giving him the forever home he always dreamed of, he was ripped away from the only person he ever loved and trusted. I was confident in this one thing: I was an absolute failure with nothing of value to offer.

Cut down. Hurt. Exposed. Useless. Unable to move.

With shattered dreams, a broken heart, no friends and no church, we struggled as a family to survive. The crisis of losing our son spiraled into possible financial ruin, counseling for our children and for my diagnosis of post-traumatic stress disorder, marital issues and more.

There were many times I might have preferred to hide in the woods, be taken away in pieces with the rest of myself or be ground into the dirt and just be done with it all.

Many days I struggled to even get out of bed. I missed my son so much and ached for the pain I knew he was experiencing. His new foster dad felt it best to have a brand-new start and allowed no contact in person, verbal or written. I truly mourned as if he had died. Overwhelmed with feelings of failure and blaming myself for the hurt my other children and extended family experienced, I pulled back, built walls and barely functioned. But I couldn't stay in bed. As silly as it might sound, I was obligated to show up at the craft shows I had booked, and so I did. I had recently joined a company called Lilla Rose and was selling unique and beautiful hair clips. I would hold up mirrors to show the women how they looked and over and over they would light up and smile seeing themselves so pretty. In that situation, I felt forced to put on a happy face and forget about my troubles. I began to treasure those moments of focusing on others and not on my loss and pain. Minutes without crying turned into hours, and hours into days. However insignificant it may have seemed to some, I was helping people. And if felt good! Other ladies started to enroll with the company and suddenly there were women across the country who had questions and needed help. In all honestly, I didn't have a clue what I was doing! I was brand new to direct sales. Without experience, knowledge or even any confidence, I just began giving them the only thing I had left to offer. Myself. ***Sprout!***

I poured myself into my growing team. Years went by.

Then one day…I looked up.

And then…I looked back.

And I realized I wasn't that cut down, useless stump anymore!

It was like the day I walked onto our front lawn and gasped in disbelief, "Willow! You've grown back! How is that possible? You were dead! You were cut down to nothing! And now? Well, look at you, Willow! All full of new life, beautiful branches and leaves!" ***Bloom!***

I didn't notice as Willow's new branches were bursting up out of that stump. But once she was grown again, you couldn't miss her! I guess that's kind of how it happened for me too.

How did Willow and I grow back after being cut down to the stump?

And more importantly, how can you?

Your story might not look exactly like mine. It doesn't matter how different we are, where you are in your life right now, how badly you've been hurt or how strongly you believe you are a failure. When we get down to the root of it, a lie is a lie. It's a lie that you are a failure. And the truth is the truth. The truth doesn't change. The truth is *you are valuable*!

Even cut down to the stump, Willow's roots were still there! Now I know, all that time, deep down, so were mine! And you know what? So are *yours!* At our core, our roots, we are all valuable. Our value is comprised of two types: intrinsic and market value. As stated by Bob Burg, coauthor of *The Go-Giver,* "Intrinsic value means that just by virtue of being born we bring great value to the world." Psalms 139:14 says, "I praise you, for I am fearfully and wonderfully made. Wonderful are your works; my soul knows it very well." We are intrinsically valuable because God made us wonderful! Bob describes our market value this way: "Those strengths, traits, talents and characteristics that allow you to add value to others, to the world, to the marketplace in such a way that you will be financially compensated for it." I believe God led me, through the following steps I'll share, to people and opportunities that helped me see and believe in my value again.

We all need certain things to stay alive and to heal and grow again when we've been cut down. Below are six things that significantly helped me.

Though action steps can be extremely helpful for focus and practical application, if too long, complicated or overly challenging, those of us already struggling with believing in our value will quit before we've even begun. My steps are simple. When the first item is checked off the list, you will feel a sense of accomplishment and be encouraged that your day is already off to a great start! You'll move on and accomplish steps two through six! Step one is your gimmee. Just wake up.

1: Wake up—remember the soil!

Be thankful for another day. A fresh start in the soil you are planted in. Like a tree's roots, the soil you are currently planted in is not typically a factor you can quickly change. Plants require different soil conditions to do well. Sometimes we assume we can put any plant in any soil and it will grow and thrive. That's not true. At different points in your life, maybe right now, you might find yourself planted in soil—conditions of life—that impacts your ability to thrive. Maybe even your belief that you can survive. You might not be able to change the soil you are planted in right now, but steps two through six are going to help you with certain things that you can learn to control so that you can flourish into the beautiful woman you were created to be!

2: Get up—consider the sun!

You've checked off step one. That's awesome! But you can't just stay in bed. I know, it is terribly tempting some days. But your value and your contributions to the world are too crucial to keep hidden under the covers. It's a brand-new day and you've got this! Just like the sun provides the warmth and energy for Willow to grow, you need to purposely find what will warm you up and give you energy to make the most of each day. I love the silly-sounding, but absolutely astounding idea from Zig Ziglar's book *See You at the Top*. As soon as you open your eyes, sit up in your bed, clap your hands and excitedly say something like, "Oh boy! Today is going to be fabulous! I can't wait to get up and take advantage of all the opportunities the world has to offer!" Will you feel stupid? I guarantee it! Then you'll laugh! There aren't many better ways to begin your day than with laughter! Have a playlist of your favorite, upbeat, get-you-going songs loaded and turn up the volume! You won't be able to stop your feet from tapping and you'll feel better when you begin your day dancing. You are making a conscious choice to refuse to start your day listening to lies and instead warming up your mind with positive thoughts and energy. Write down three things that you *can* do. Nothing you think you can't. Tape it on your bathroom mirror and read it each morning. Add to the list as you realize more and more things you can do. You are *not* a failure! And you are going to have an amazing day!

3: Show up—don't forget to water!

You are awake and out of bed. So far, so good! Now, you need to be brave. You need to show up. Show up for events, obligations, meetings, work and social opportunities. When we believe we are a failure with nothing of value to offer, we stop showing up to life. Depending on how long you've been isolating yourself from people and responsibilities, others may have stopped inviting you to events. You might need to invite yourself or create your own opportunities to show up to life. Willow needed water to grow new branches and leaves, and so do you! The water represents the constant flow of life. Pouring into you and from you into others. For me, the start was the vendor events. Forcing myself to be around others played a crucial role in my healing and learning to believe in my value again. Beyond just showing up for the basics of life, I would encourage you to show up for specific events that are designed to teach you something new, motivate you and encourage you to action! Surround yourself with uplifting people. Purposely seek out friends and family who will speak kind and encouraging words into your life. Avoid anyone and any group—even on social media—that is negative. Show up for opportunities to fill your mind with positive and valuable thoughts. Reading inspiring books is a great alternative when there isn't a specific event or gathering you could attend. (Hey! Check you out! You are doing that right now!)

4: Build others up—imagine the possibilities with fertilizer!

Self-pity and isolation are fertilizer for lies. The longer you focus on your problems, the more food you are feeding the lie that you are a failure and have nothing of value to offer.

On the contrary, encouraging and building *others* up and helping them believe in their value is fertilizer for believing in *your* own value. What a tremendous surprise when I realized that while I was sprouting back to life, finding my own way to believing in myself again, I was helping other ladies do the same! The same fertilizer that feeds your beliefs will, in turn, by its very nature, be encouraging others to believe that they too are valuable! Author Jill Briscoe says, "Be encouraged to be an encourager. It's a spiritual art that everyone can learn. And mostly you learn by practicing it."

5: Don't blow up—take a deep breath of fresh air!

Let's face it, no one enjoys confrontation, obstacles, roadblocks, hurt feelings or misunderstandings. But everyone faces these problems, so what should we do? Tony Robbins says it best when he says, "In life, never spend more than ten percent of your time on the problem, and spend at least ninety percent of your time on the solution."

Here's the bottom line. Bad stuff happens. Life isn't fair. People can be mean. You will make mistakes. Things break. When you recognize and accept that things will break, but you refuse to let that break you, it's like breathing fresh air on a pollution-filled day! When people hurt or upset you, and they will, don't blow up. Take a deep breath and go back to step four. I mentioned that my steps were "simple," but I never said they were all going to be easy! Focus at least ninety percent of your time on solutions, moving forward and what you can control.

6: Don't ever give up—even when pruning is necessary!

Even trees don't continue to grow beyond their ability to support and maintain themselves. There will be times when you realize that you are overstressed, in over your head, struggling to cope or mourning a loss. During those times, try to recognize that what feels painful in the moment is the loss of branches you could no longer support. You are pruning leaves, fruit, flowers and branches that are dying. Prune, but never give in or give up!

Loss, hardship and a vast array of obstacles can make life difficult to navigate. You might be fully in your right to blame your past, present hurts and even some mistakes on others. But your future, starting with this very moment, is on you! Decide today that you are not going to remain what you have been cut down to! Allow the pruning and even severe cuts to shape you into a better you! The best and most valuable you!

It's time to grow again, Willow! Time to sprout new, beautiful leaves! To stand tall and share your oasis of value with everyone around you! Because of its ability to spring back to life, even when severely cut down, the willow tree has been cherished as a symbol of immortality and renewal. My Willow grew back into an even more beautiful and valuable tree than before. I grew into a more beautiful and valuable me! We're both planning on staying this way for a very long time. I hope you'll let my willow tree, and my story, be an example of tremendous potential for *you* to be renewed and become all that you are and all that you are destined to become!

Shannon Ferraby

When Shannon is not a hundred feet under, scuba diving in caves or with sharks, she's on a mission! A mission to stop women from listening to and believing lies that are holding them back from who they were created to be! Lies whispering, "You aren't good enough." "You don't have what it takes." Sometimes shouting, "You are a failure!"

As a certified Go-Giver speaker, trainer and coach, she believes and teaches that the most valuable gift you can offer is yourself! Shannon is known for giving "Daily KIPs," a phrase she coined to describe her loving but firm "Kick In the Pants" to encourage and motivate ladies to action!

Shannon is the highest-ranking leader in Lilla Rose, Inc., a hair accessory and solutions company. She passionately leads, trains and coaches thousands of women. Shannon has personally developed over twenty-five unique training's, has been a speaker for annual conventions, weekly live training calls and creates and leads the company's regional workshops. A wife of over twenty-four years, homeschooling mommy to five and children's ministry director for her church, Shannon is proof that even a tree cut down to the stump can grow again and flourish to greatness!

Shannon Ferraby
PO Box 1896
Hiram, OH 44234
330-569-8580
shannon@shannonferraby.com
www.lillarose.biz/greateights
www.shannonferraby.com
www.facebook.com/groups/believinginyourvalue

Lynn O'Dowd

Unleash Your Inner Superstar

Get this: in a moment of madness I answered an ad to be a singer in a rock 'n' roll band after not singing for over thirty-five years. In those thirty-five years, I enjoyed a successful career, eighteen years of which I spent as a time management/organizing consultant in the business and corporate marketplace. I taught, looked like and lived traditional structure, even naming my company All About Time.

I always thought this was my main "gift," being a productivity expert. Truth be told, I often felt that I had been short-changed in the talent department because I was only okay at other things, and didn't excel at them as easily as I did at organizing and time management. I never took time to pursue, develop or cultivate any of my "lesser" talents. I compared myself to others who were more successful in those areas and knew I would never be that good. I also made the assumption that my "okay" gifts and talents would not earn me money or make me more successful. So, I figured, *Why even try developing them?*

I couldn't have been more wrong.

Recognize All Your Gifts

In order to achieve the success, happiness and fulfillment you desire, you must recognize ALL your gifts, the God-given natural talents you have had inside you since you were born. What many people may not realize is that all of the gifts and talents you need to succeed are already INSIDE YOU! They are unique to you, so that no one can express them the way you can.

Sadly, we often spend our entire lives with our gifts hidden, under-utilized or fighting against them. And until we recognize and utilize all of our gifts, it can be difficult to realize our full potential.

All Gifts Great and Small

The gift that I had hidden, ignored and fought against—I call this "the trifecta"—was performing. I did not think I was good enough. I really believed that I'd never be a rock star performer, so why bother?

My lack of confidence was nurtured when, as a child, I was called a show-off by both family and friends, and the word performer took on a negative connotation for me. Little did I know that all of us need to show off our talents; some on a big stage, some on a small stage and some back stage. Sometimes, we resist our gifts out of fear, but sometimes, it's simply a case of being uninformed.

What I didn't realize at the time is that it's the combination of all your talents, great and small, that make up the whole of you. When you embrace your whole being and know who you truly are, it empowers you and gives you a sense of fulfillment and a feeling of completeness. And when you own your personal power, you are able to apply it to every aspect of your life and business, as well as step outside of your comfort zone and risk new levels of passion.

Your Gifts Are for You and All the Lives You Touch

Another important lesson I've come to realize is that your gifts are not just about you. They are about all the lives you touch. Others need our natural-born abilities to organize, manage, strategize, sell, teach, entertain, make music, provide compassion or a listening ear.

Take a few moments and think about YOUR gifts. What makes you uniquely brilliant? Which do you use to carry you and others forward? Which ones are you not using or afraid to develop? What's stopping you from using ALL of your natural gifts and talents?

Recently, I read this quote on Facebook, and it rings true for many people I know: *"The meaning of life is to discover your gifts, and the purpose is to give them away."*

Super Stuck to Superstar

Oftentimes, before you can unleash the superstar within you and live the life of your dreams, you go through a phase of feeling super stuck. We all have had the feeling of being stuck at some point in our lives. The everyday busyness of our lives doesn't help; day in, day out, same ol', same ol'. I liken it to the same song playing in our head over and over; same tune, same lyrics, same old ideas and, oftentimes, the same limitations.

I didn't start out feeling like I was stuck. I just thought I was comfortable. As time went on, it became extremely uncomfortable because I knew I could be more, and I couldn't shake the uninspired feeling. Do not mistake comfort for happiness.

Getting "Unstuck" is an Inner Game

Being stuck is not about what's happening to us. It's an inner issue. I learned this lesson the hard way, over the course of many years. I often blamed my "stuckness" on something outside of me: my job, lack of money, time, resources and let's not forget my husband—an easy target to blame! I changed some of these outside influences—I changed jobs, careers, income, and even tried to change my husband's actions by always telling him what to do. That didn't go so well! I felt better for a while, but the reality was I was still singing the same ol' song, just at a different venue. My mentor summed it up nicely: *"When we think we have limits, we sometimes create them."*

So, the first step I took was to recognize the change needing to happen within me. I realized that if I wanted to have the time of my life, I was going to have to make some changes inside of me. This was the best thing that could have happened, although it didn't feel like it at the time. This introspection allowed me to examine my priorities, values, heart-centered issues and, ultimately, opened a door for a change in perspective to occur.

Change Requires Action—Time to Act!

Of course, the next questions were what and how to change. At that point,
I had no idea of the answer. All I knew was that doing the same thing was only
going to continue giving me the same results. So, I started by doing something
different. Doing something different, outside of your normal routine, allows
you to view your life and the world in a completely new way. In order to get
started, you don't have to know where you are headed, just take the first step.
In my case, I chose something different that I knew I would enjoy. I started
singing again!

I hadn't sung in over thirty-five years, since I finished school. I figured it
wasn't going to get me ahead in life or make me more successful, so I stopped
singing entirely. In order to get back in the swing of things, I started off by
singing in the car, shower and while I was exercising. Although I had doubts
about how this was going to get me further in life, I kept going and asked
myself, *What else can I do other than sing in the shower?* I couldn't see the
whole way ahead, only one or two steps in front of me, but I put my faith in that
because that was all I could do at the time. Anything more felt overwhelming
and difficult. The key is to be one hundred percent committed to taking the
next small step.

Be Flexible and Try

Once you've made the decision and put yourself on the path, your next
step is to be flexible and just try. The path may not be exactly right, and the steps
may at first seem unclear, but when you are committed to self-improvement,
to making changes in your life, the next step will reveal itself in time. I came
across this paraphrased quote from Joseph Campbell, *"When you follow your
bliss, doors will open where there were none."*

That is how it worked for me. I was thumbing through the newspaper
and an ad jumped out at me: *Come be a singer in a rock 'n' roll band.* My heart
stopped! Singer in a band? Now that would be fun! My mind immediately
jumped to, *I could be a rock star, the next Lady Gaga, my favorite singer.* But

in the next moment, I squelched all those exciting thoughts and let doubt creep in by thinking, *Who am I to be a singer in a band? I'm not that good. This is just for young people. Besides, the last time I sang on stage I was sixteen in the high school talent show!* So, I immediately put the newspaper down and walked away from the ad.

Except I couldn't get that stinkin' ad out of my head! For three days it was constantly on my mind. Do you want to know why I couldn't get it out of my head? Because your bliss never leaves you, you leave it. For me, it was singing and answering the ad. What is it for you? What is it that you can't seem to shake from your mind or your heart? What has been calling you for years but for some reason or another you have been afraid to pick up? Chances are that's your happiness.

Eventually, I gave in and answered the ad, knowing that I couldn't live with myself if I didn't try. When I went to the audition, I was scared out of my mind! I was way beyond my comfort zone. But I took the chance anyway, because what was the worst that could happen? I could be laughed at, embarrassed or escorted off stage. So, I sang my heart out to Lady Gaga's song "Born This Way." The first line, "We are all born superstars," came out shaky but I kept singing.

And guess what? I got in the band! Perhaps even more unbelievable was that the name of the band was LTD: Living the Dream. Here I was, looking to live my dream, and that was the name of the band! You see, when you follow your bliss, you tap into your gifts, and your mind begins to open up to solutions, possibilities and opportunities that help you find what you have been looking for.

Sometimes Your "Stuck Point" Comes Before Your Turning Point

Where are you right now in your life? Where do you want to be? What do you need to make that happen? If you desire to achieve something different than where you are right now, to go from being super stuck to a superstar, then thinking about it is not enough. You must take action. You are never going to

FEEL ready to do something you're afraid of; it's all about getting out of your comfort zone and taking action.

We all know we can just exist and go through the motions. However, if you are reading this, there's likely a part of you that knows you are capable of more, that you are capable of playing on a bigger stage. I have both witnessed it in others and experienced it myself: there is always a moment of transformation, a turning point, not external but rather something internal that tells you today is THE DAY. NOW is the moment to take action on what you truly desire to achieve.

Sometimes you know what to do next, but you don't take action due to excuses—the next step feels too hard, too icky, or you're too tired, too busy. Or, sometimes you feel you know you need to make changes to achieve your desires, but you just don't know what changes you need to make. That's difficult, isn't it? The only way change happens is by you taking action, because doing the same thing will give you the same results. Are you ready for that change?

You have nothing to lose and everything to gain. It wasn't easy for me—I was afraid to answer the ad, afraid to audition and afraid the night of my first performance. I couldn't see the whole way ahead of me but I kept putting one foot in front of the other, experimenting with what made me happy, and before I knew it, I was enjoying life fully again. Looking back, I realize that sometimes your stuck point comes right before your turning point, and that turning point can give you the time of your life!

From Rock 'n' Roll Singer to Motivational Speaker & Keynote Performer

When I became a rock 'n' roll singer at the age of fifty-two, everyone wanted to hear HOW I did it, and wished they could live their dreams too. I realized there are so many people in the world who want to play a bigger game and make a bigger difference in their life and work, yet they often never get to fulfill any of their dreams due to fear, lack of self-worth or perhaps the negative voice playing in their head.

So, I decided to do something about it.

I became a motivational speaker and corporate keynote performer and created a unique, energizing and transformational keynote just for them. I combine the power of heart-opening music, live guitar-playing and soul-stirring singing with engaging storytelling, personal inspiration and a truly unforgettable finale where I unleash my inner superstar and transform into Lady Gaga right before their eyes. I help audiences step out of their comfort zone and risk new levels of passion, performance and courage in business and life.

In a nutshell, I move them from I CAN'T to I CAN! in sixty minutes or less using my GoGaGa™ formula.

Lessons Learned at the Lady Gaga Concert

As you can see in this photo, I literally demonstrate transformation on stage. I have been a fan of Lady Gaga for some time now. The ol' disco queen in me loves her dance music. I also personally admire her because she doesn't hold back in life; she lives her name and "goes gaga." So, when I learned she was coming to Chicago to play at Wrigley Field, I immediately jumped online to get tickets.

Fear Disguised as Practicality

I had heard and seen photos on social media that Lady Gaga's fans, called "Little Monsters," dressed up in a variety of Lady Gaga's costumes at her concerts. The thought of that seemed like so much fun to me. However, my inner critic was swirling in my head as to whether I should go to the concert in a Gaga costume. I thought, *Will anyone else, or anyone fifty-six years old, be wearing a costume? Dressing up is for young people, and I'll embarrass myself.* I was feeling very self-conscious and very self-judgmental, but I couldn't let it go. I couldn't stop thinking, *What is stopping me from going full out at the concert?* The answer was what has stopped me many other times in my life: the rules that were made up for me by society, authority, family, friends and myself as to what I could or could not do. Dressing up wouldn't be the adult, responsible, practical thing to do, right? All this worry was fear disguised as practicality. How often do you talk yourself out of things you are really inspired to do?

Concert day came. As I dressed in my "regular" clothes, I felt disappointed. I felt disappointed with my plain outfit, in myself that I was chickening out on wearing the costume and being true to how I wanted to show up that night: the flashy, outrageous GoGaGa™ Lynn — my disco queen inner superstar. As the tears started to bubble up, I switched gears fast and listened to my heart. Out came the silver glitter, bling, spiked heels, leather and Gaga wig. I was not going to disappoint Mother Monster, so I went for it full out.

Mosh Pit or "Safe" Seats

When I got to Wrigley Field, a miracle happened — a staff member pulled me to the side and asked me, and even my husband, if we would like to stand in front of the stage. I thought it was some type of scam since this area is difficult to get tickets for no matter how much you pay. Doubt set in for me because this was so unbelievable. She was asking us to stand in the mosh pit. I'd never been in a mosh pit. Would there be pushing and shoving during the entire show? Was she really telling the truth? I was debating staying in my comfort zone of what I knew and had always known — the "safe" seats — or risking the mosh pit. Sometimes saying YES to what you really want takes courage. I thought, *What would Lady Gaga do?* Mosh pit!

We were whisked through security into an underground tunnel and walked to the very front of the stage with all the other dressed up Little Monsters. I was stage front BECAUSE I dressed up FULL OUT. All Little Monsters in costume were recruited to go up front to support Lady Gaga in her performance. I fit right in! Another Little Monster overheard my husband say, "I think we're the oldest ones in this mosh pit." The millennial turned to me and said, "You make all of us look better, and you lift us all to a higher standard. You are beautiful. Thank you." A message from the heart. It's not always easy to step into your true, authentic self, but when you do, doors open and miracles can happen.

Are You Playing Full Out in Your Life?

What I learned at this concert was that participating full out in your business, in your personal life or at a Lady Gaga concert, even with doubts, gives others permission to do the same for themselves. Your courage gives others courage. It opens doors to opportunities you never thought possible or perhaps even dreamed of. I shut down my negative self-talk and followed my heart, and as a result, ended up front row, center stage, having the time of my life because I took a chance and dared to be ME!

That night, Lady Gaga performed full out, and gave us everything she had for the entire show for all her fans, her Little Monsters. It was a night of inspiration, music, dance, love, fun and compassion for all. Truly, an uplifting experience. That night I sang, I screamed, I danced, I laughed, I cried and I looked Lady Gaga right in the eye as she sang to me, *"You were born this way, baby!"*

And so were you.

Don't be afraid to embrace all your gifts and take the first step towards your dreams in business and life.

It's often said that our biggest regrets in life are about what we didn't try or do rather than what we did try and didn't work out. It's a decision to live a life that is more than just going through the motions. Take it from me, it's worth the decision to step out of your comfort zone and unleash YOUR inner superstar!

Unleash Your Inner Superstar™

"Step out of your comfort zone and risk

new levels of passion, performance and courage."

—Lynn O'Dowd—

Motivational Speaker & Keynote Performer

www.LynnODowd.com

Lynn O'Dowd

Motivational Speaker & Keynote Performer

Lynn O'Dowd has overcome thyroid cancer, walked on forty feet of burning hot coals, and successfully run her own organizing business for over eighteen years. However, none of this compares to the personal challenge she set for herself of going way outside of her comfort zone to experience life and perform at levels she never thought possible. Armed with her GoGaGa™ formula, the transformational process she developed to help her overcome fear and achieve extraordinary success, Lynn redefined middle age and leaped from being a successful corporate time management consultant to being a rock 'n' roll singer and inspirational keynote speaker!

Today, Lynn's highly-entertaining keynote combines the transformational power of heart-opening music, live guitar-playing, and soul-stirring singing with engaging storytelling, personal inspiration, and a truly unforgettable finale where she "Unleashes Her Inner Superstar" and transforms into Lady Gaga right before your eyes. She inspires audiences to step out of their comfort zone to risk new levels of passion, performance and courage. She equips people with the know-how to "Unleash Their Inner Superstar" with the realization that it's never too late to bust through their fears to achieve their full potential for greater success and happiness in business and life!

Lynn is a professional motivational speaker, keynote performer, certified professional organizer and time management consultant. She combines her strong track record in self-motivation, personal development and keynote performance, with her equally strong business background, outstanding time management and process development expertise to help individuals and organizations accomplish their BIGGEST goals and dreams. She is a graduate of Northern Illinois University, the Covey Leadership program, the LifeSpring personal development leadership program and has been a workshop facilitator for Anthony Robbins and John Gray, Ph.D., Mars Venus workshops.

Lynn is a member of the National Speakers Association, Windy City Professional Speakers, National Association of Productivity & Organizing Professionals and the National Customer Service Association.

"Unleash Your Inner Superstar™"
Demo Video: www.youtube.com/watch?v=FQ78NrMxeVM
www.facebook.com/lynn.odowd
www.linkedin.com/in/lynnmeyerodowd
@LynnGoGaGa

Lynn O'Dowd
Motivational Speaker & Keynote Performer
4320 N. Mason Ave.
Chicago, IL 60634
312-498-1857
Lynn@LynnODowd.com
www.LynnODowd.com

Jackie Schwabe

Finding Balance in Chaos—Juggling Birds

The Greatest Show on Earth—It's All an Act

My mother was an addict and alcoholic when I was growing up. Mother had various boyfriends and more than a few husbands over the years, many of varied morality and humanity. At one of my mother's lowest points, we lived in her car in the middle of winter in Michigan. In spite of it all, it seemed like I had overcome the obstacles of my upbringing and succeeded. I went to college and received two advanced degrees. I married a wonderful man from a nice Catholic family. We had an honest to goodness Catholic wedding, and God didn't strike the church with lightning. I had three beautiful children and one more bundle of joy on the way. I also had two four-legged children, our Husky, Kovu, and our Pomeranian, Sammie, who brought us comfort and joy. I had my dream job, the director of innovation, at a cutting edge small company making cardiac MRI visualization software. I was juggling a marriage, children, and a demanding career, and from the outside looking in, things looked pretty darn great. Everyone thought I had it all together.

What they didn't see was my life was out of balance and it was soon to be catapulted into chaos. I don't ascribe to the whole work-life balance theory: fifty percent of your time should be at work and fifty percent of your time should be at home. Every day lends itself to a different ratio. I am not Lady Justice, sometimes I am juggling twenty balls in the air and trying to make sure none of the glass balls fall and break. I don't have the luxury of a scale with only two options to weigh. The ratio for me was more like ten percent home and ninety percent work. Chaos seeks balance, so the universe intervened.

Thankfully, I was forced to create a healthier lifestyle.

Learning to Juggle—Don't Drop the Balls

August 5, 2013: I was carrying my third child, Zoe, on top of my very pregnant belly to an Autism evaluation; the new baby, who we called Jack Jack, was due September 11, 2013. You might wonder why I would carry a nearly two-year-old child—Zoe refused to walk, didn't talk, and was fond of darting out in front of danger with no worry for her safety. This appointment was the last of many, targeted at finding out why she did such things; it was also the first day of our next journey.

I thought the two-hour evaluation went well, since my non-verbal child said her first word: bird. Bird wasn't mommy, but it was a start. The woman who evaluated my little angel said, "She is at least moderately autistic." Just like that. Okay. I had one more ball to juggle.

Then the woman informed me how our life was about to change. Zoe would need forty hours a week of one-on-one, in home ABA therapy. But the therapist could not be in our home without another adult present. A session could not exceed two hours, and may or may not run concurrently. Zoe would need this therapy until she was old enough to go to school and receive services through the special education system. Insurance may not cover the costs, but if it did, there would likely be a copayment per session. They had an opening for Zoe in their schedule. Did I want the opening? And how would I be paying for the services?

"But she said bird," was all I could say. I dropped Zoe off at home with our daycare person and returned to the office. I shut the door and sobbed.

Less than a month after the diagnosis, my then four-year-old son, Max, started 4K at a new school. My oldest, Ava, was going into second grade. I held Zoe on my belly as I tried to hold Max's hand and introduce him to his new teacher. That was the start of his journey with dyslexia. I had one more ball to juggle.

Well, fate is a female dog. The daycare person felt we lied to her when she was hired since we didn't tell her about Zoe's diagnosis. She was hired in June, and Zoe's diagnosis was in August. The presumed lie heightened tensions in an already fragile household. She also didn't like dogs. I suspect out of frustration and in a constant state of overwhelm, which I could relate to, she left our dogs outside on a hot day and Sammie died of heat stroke. Kovu went a little off his rocker, missing his partner of thirteen years, and soon followed his friend over the rainbow bridge. I had one more ball to juggle.

Elephants Sure Do Work Hard—The Struggles Continue

On September 11, 2013, while I was delivering the new baby, I was trying to juggle my career in the chaos. "Just one more text message. I have to make sure the guys know what to do when I am out on maternity leave," I said to my husband, Mark. It is a miracle he didn't divorce me. In the middle of a contraction, thankfully a medicated one, I was texting the office. Jack Jack arrived sooner than expected, so the hospitalist, not the OB, ended up delivering him. The OB showed up just in time to stitch me up. Stitches suck, especially, well, you know. I was in a hurry to get out of the hospital as I needed to catch up on work, schedule therapy and dyslexia appointments, resolve the daycare conflict, and console our children after the loss of our pets. I should have stayed an extra few days. It was the last break I would get for a very long time.

I was 245 pounds after delivering Jack Jack, the most I ever weighed. My blood pressure was high, due to the pregnancy, but I was sure the weight didn't help. I was thirty-six years old, of advanced maternal age, the OB often reminded me. At my six-week post-partum check-up, I reiterated my constant battle with fatigue. Tons of tests later, the sleep specialist diagnosed me with narcolepsy. I had one more ball to juggle.

The Lion Bites the Lion Tamer—Hitting Rock Bottom

A few weeks before Christmas, my dream job was taken from me. They said my position was eliminated; the new guy started the Monday after I left. I suspected all my healthcare expenses didn't positively affect their self-funded insurance plan's bottom line. They told me if I signed the separation papers immediately, I could keep my health insurance until March. I needed the insurance. I had more balls to juggle.

Later that week, I got the call that my mother was in ICU. The doctors weren't sure if she would live through the night. I was her designated medical power of attorney. My stepfather, who I am closest with, had a heart attack. My father, the biological one, was diagnosed with congestive heart failure and COPD. At the same time, we continued to reassure our daycare person we didn't intend to deceive her, but she left on her own just short of a year after she started. I had more balls to juggle.

The Show Must Go On

You might think this story is tragic or maybe feel bad for me. The truth is, my story isn't as uncommon as you might think. Everyone, whether you know it or not, is going through some type of difficult experience. I knew I couldn't juggle any more balls, something had to change. That pivotal moment came from an unsuspecting source, my daughter Zoe.

I was so focused on my career that I did not take the time to enjoy my family. I had four beautiful children, each with their own unique gifts to share with the world. Since Mark and I miscarried four times, you would think I would have been more thankful for the gift of my children's lives. I wasn't the type of person who took first day of school pictures or cried as they got on the bus. Honestly, I was relieved they went to school—they were the school's responsibility for a while. I certainly didn't pay attention to the date that they took their first steps or when they spoke their first words. They were supposed to do all of those things. Well, typically developing children did, but I had a child who was not typical. I had a neurologically divergent child.

The Only Way to Improve Your Performance is to Act—The Turning Point

As I observed Zoe during her daily therapy sessions, I began to notice how complex learning was. Learning wasn't just complex for Zoe; everyone learned in his or her own way and at their own pace. The simple act of potty training for Zoe, something my older children did easily, had to be broken down into many small steps. I realized life wasn't just about reaching major milestones. Life was about the many small steps, the journey. So, each time she went to the bathroom and used the potty, we celebrated. I finally learned how to celebrate life. It was so much easier to celebrate in small steps, especially since I avoided doing it for so long.

I eventually found another job. The new job allowed me to work from home, with occasional travel. It wasn't my dream job, but it helped me manage my new, chaotic life. Frankly, the occasional travel was much needed. The travel breaks allowed the time for my next realization to strike. I had casually pursued starting my own company in the past, but nothing serious ever developed. I told myself I didn't have any valuable skills. I didn't realize we were all given divine gifts. I now feel we are given gifts from God that we are meant to share, and it is our obligation to do so. I didn't realize the things that came easily to me were my gifts: researching problems, finding unique solutions, connecting disparate ideas and people, and organizing chaos. These things were simple to me, but they were not simple to others. I overlooked my own skills because I was good at them. I assumed everyone else was good at them as well.

Clowns Make You Laugh—You've Got to Be You

I also realized that I had always been a helper. I am that person who gives money to homeless people. Friends would caution me, "Homeless people will probably drink away their sorrows with your money." I always replied, "Once a gift is given, it is no longer your decision on how it is used." I was disappointed in myself. God gave me all these skills and gifts, and I was wasting them away with self-doubt. It may have no longer been God's decision on how I used my gifts, but I suspected he was pretty darn disappointed I was selfishly hoarding them. I had an obligation to share my time, talent, and treasure with those in need. I was able to reconnect with my faith through this simple epiphany. My faith had been one hundred percent missing from my work-life balance ratio. By adding faith back into the equation, I was reducing the balls I was juggling. I was able to drop guilt and self-doubt. I knew I was headed on the right path.

I also gained the insight that habits are tools we need to gain new skills and establish expertise. Again, Zoe taught me this lesson. She woke up every day at 7:00 a.m. She went to bed at 8:00 p.m. She was never tired during the day. Her routine was solid. She may have been a girl of few words, but her actions spoke volumes. Without an alarm clock to wake her, she opened her eyes and started her day promptly at 7:00 a.m. Zoe started chaining habits together, connecting each step to allow her to learn things previously unobtainable. A timer prompted her to go to the bathroom. The timer also trained us to remind her it was potty time. Zoe's habit chains even trained us! I celebrated each of her successes.

Tightrope Walkers are Scared — But They Do it Anyway

Shortly after the habit chains principle was integrated into my life came the awareness that everyone is afraid of something, not just me. So, if everyone was afraid, then being scared was not a weakness, but a condition of humanity. In fact, feeling fear could be a good thing. If you feel fear, you have a built-in trigger that tells you to act. Fear is the external manifestation of our fight-or-flight instincts. One thing that sets us apart from the rest of mammals, in my opinion, is we are warned by our feelings, giving us enough time to process a more effective response. The warning allows us to make the conscious decision of whether to fight or flee. To me, this meant if I felt fear, I could plan for how to overcome it. Having a plan meant I had more control. Most importantly, I learned that being courageous wasn't about blindly stepping into the pathway of danger; being courageous was being afraid of danger and choosing a safer and smarter way to do it anyway.

I can't think of a more courageous person than Zoe, and she is only six years old. She is afraid to speak, yet she learned to talk. She is afraid of loud noises, but she learned to cover her ears. She is afraid of cars, and bugs, and dogs, and people. Yet she goes outside every day where there are cars, bugs, dogs, and people. She is afraid of the potty, yet she goes in several times a day. She is afraid of so many things, yet she is strong enough to do them anyway. She is the most courageous person I know, and if she can be brave, so can I.

All these insights gave me the courage to take action. I lost over sixty-five pounds and have kept it off, in spite of having narcolepsy, which increases hunger. I started by creating small, positive habits and chaining them together. First, I started to drink more water. Then, I started to reduce my soda intake. I replaced not eating breakfast with drinking a meal replacement shake. I began walking after dinner with Mark. I added vitamin supplements. I started incorporating essential oils into my daily routine. Little by little, I chained together small things and got big results. There were setbacks, or so I thought. I initially lost eighty pounds, but as I started engaging in other activities like kickboxing, the result was gaining weight. I panicked, and then recalled I was celebrating making healthy choices step by step. The numbers on the scale, my old goal, no longer had power over me. It's been four years since I started the journey and I still feel great.

I spent those same four years struggling to find the resources and tools to support Zoe and my mother. I was frustrated. It took me over three months to find the necessary support services for my mom. I am still trying to navigate the system for Zoe as she continues to develop and her needs change. A problem was staring me right in the face, but this time, I was ready to take action. The inability to find the information I needed to support my family was a problem. I was going to turn those lemons into lemonade.

The Final Act—Learning to Juggle Birds

On January 4, 2017, I launched a business focused on helping others find the resources they need. I wouldn't have been able to do this before Zoe's diagnosis changed my life. I had to realize and accept that my unique skills had value. I had to be brave and overcome my fear of selling and rejection. I had to accept that my natural desire to help was a passion, a calling that I needed to heed. I had to accept the gifts I was given and share them. I was afraid to fail, but this time, I knew fear was a trigger. I used the trigger to plan, and a business plan was the result. The business plan convinced an investor to believe in me as much as I now believe in myself. I can sell.

Chaining habits together made the largest impact on my productivity. I needed to gain the above insights for my mental health, but I still needed a way to manage the continued injections of chaos into my life. My journey to getting healthier was the first success. Writing daily was the second. I learned if I don't have to think about a task and just do it automatically, I am less tempted to get off track. Chaining habits together allowed me to forgo using the energy required to make a million decisions a day because the decisions were made when I chose to include them into my habit chain. I stopped juggling balls and started juggling birds. Establishing habits turned balls into birds; it was glorious.

Zoe still has an autism diagnosis. Max still has dyslexia. My mother is still hanging on by a thread. My father still has COPD and CHF. My stepfather now has emphysema as well as heart problems. I still have narcolepsy. We have two new dogs, Ollie and Tyron. I am still married to Mark, thank God. Recently, my mother-in-law was diagnosed with Parkinson's. I am the CEO of MindLight, LLC. I am a volleyball coach and Girl Scout leader. I volunteer at my children's school and our church. I am writing a book. The balls I am juggling now are not much different than they were four years ago, except the ones I turned into habits are more like juggling birds.

My work-life ratio is more balanced now, rarely ninety percent work, ten percent family. I celebrate small moments every day and value my gifts. I feel my fear and do what scares me anyway. But mostly, I watch for lessons taught by children. I look for lessons you can only learn by participating in their lives and hearing their first words, even if their first word is bird. Zoe knew it all along—I needed to stop jugging balls and start juggling birds. Darn, that kid is smart.

Jackie Schwabe

Jackie Schwabe is CEO of MindLight, LLC and vice president of leadership research at North of Center. She is a certified caregiving presenter, caregiving consultant, and caregiving educator. She received her BA in management computer systems from the University of Wisconsin— Whitewater and her MBA in technology project management from the University of Phoenix. She has been active in the area of healthcare integration, healthcare IT, telemedicine, product development, and product management for over twenty years. She has been a cross-sector, cross-discipline leadership practitioner her entire career.

Jackie wakes up motivated to help others. Her mission is to provide the tools, opportunities, and connections people need to be their best selves. A career in health IT allowed her to figuratively and literally connect thousands of systems and people. A mother of four children, one with autism, she often says different is not less and communication happens in more ways than verbally. She co-founded MindLight, LLC as a way to technologically help caregivers. She joined North of Center because she saw a way to use the communication-based leadership framework to help others. She is confident her roles at MindLight, LLC and North of Center will guide individuals to their best selves, and she wants to be there to help. She is a servant leader and her passion is to lead by service to others in her community.

Jackie Schwabe
MindLight, LLC
12420 W Hampton Ave #302
Butler, WI 53007
414-909-3169
jackies@mindlightllc.com
www.mindlightllc.com

Dr. Katherine "Katie" Waller

My Logical, Analytical, Creative, Crazy Life…

My life is one big case study…

Being Really Shy, and I Mean Really Shy

I learned to read and was a full-functioning reader by the age of three. I was enamored by the world of books, and as a shy child, this was my escape. Around this same time, I was introduced to the world of dance. I loved any kind of dance, including gymnastics and baton. I was usually shy at first with new children, but I was the playground leader and advocate for small, more timid kids. Adults were my biggest fear. Answering their questions and making eye contact sent me under my mom's skirt. Sensing my extreme shyness, my mom enrolled me in drama classes at my dance studio to aid in my public speaking. I can remember Ava, my teacher, saying when you are feeling shy, pretend to be someone else and have the conversation as if you were them. I always lovingly say it is amazing I did not acquire dissociative identity disorder. I have never really overcome my shyness, but my adult friends are always shocked to hear this tidbit of my childhood. I always secretly think…*thanks, Ava*.

I was blessed and cursed with an "elephant memory." Not the photographic memory that remembers every word, that I prayed for every night to help me in Chemistry class, but a memory that is more like snips of movie reels. I can remember entire conversations as if the world around me is on stage and in a play. This movie reel is sometimes extended and I play out different scenarios in my mind and I often visualize events into scenes. When I am overwhelmed, I see myself in a boat in the middle of the ocean with only one paddle, and when it is really bad, no paddles. I think it is the shyness that has me living a portion of my life in my head and keeps me half a step apart from feeling a connection with others.

Although I love deeply and intimately, I never considered myself to have tons of friends. I always felt I had a large number of people I liked and a few very close friends. As a child, it felt like I was watching myself go through life in a movie. I have kept my emotions in check and under control, with a few exceptions, so tightly that when I have swells of emotion I am surprised. I am unable to sing the National Anthem without crying. I cannot remember one time where I have made it through the entire song. I don't have a great story or parent in active service, that song just gets me every time. I can ache for a character in a book so deeply I feel they are real. But with individuals, I have kept myself so guarded from emotions and words that I feel I am in a movie and am surprised when emotions are bubbling inside. I loved being on the stage and performing, but being on a stage as myself was a huge obstacle.

So, how did I overcome this shyness? I went on to be a cheerleader and a business coach, where I sometimes presented live for hundreds of people, and even once for a thousand people. My fears and insecurities have not disappeared, and neither has my desire to live in two worlds: the life in my mind and in books, and a life involved and connected to others. It is easier to be alone and not worry about topics to discuss, but I love people—it just stresses me to talk to them. I actually gain energy from people and being around them—not having to socialize necessarily, but people—how they think, what motivates them to achieve, how some do achieve and others don't. The world is one big stage, and my life is the proverbial play within the play. Even though I was painfully shy, it didn't mean I didn't love people, so I didn't let that obstacle keep me away. I have several mantras, but one that I adopted around the age of seven is: *Everyone has something to teach you if you just watch and listen.* I think this belief is what has shaped my future the most.

Living UP to Your Potential

I have often wondered if it is worse to have no potential or to have potential and never fully reach it. As far back as I can remember, I would hear *potential* and felt more than understood the expectations implied with that word. I hated to hear "you are so pretty" as a child—I wanted to be known for being creative. I decided at the age of six that anyone who gave me a compliment about being creative or smart, I would instantly like. If they complimented my appearance, I would put them in the "I don't know" box on a shelf. This feeling lead me to the understanding that I wanted to define my legacy and not rely on others' perceptions. Therefore, I started observing the expectations of what I could accomplish. I was an above average athlete, student, dancer and gymnast. But I never actually reached my potential in any of them. I cried when I made the all-star team in softball. I say all this now not to brag or show off—as you will learn, I don't see this as great—I tell you all of this to understand the filter or filters I have placed on my world.

In seventh grade, they found a bone tumor in my knee. It turned out to be fine, but required surgery. This began a chain of events that would be my biggest obstacle and the biggest threat to reaching my potential. In the spring of eighth grade, while preparing for high school cheerleader tryouts, I injured that same knee. I actually watched as it dislocated. It was determined that I had torn cartilage in a couple of places, sprained several ligaments and surgery would be required. I still tried out, and it wasn't until the very last trick where I landed funny and hurt myself further. Regardless, surgery was three days later and the doctor was surprised my injuries had worsened. My leg was in a toe to hip cast for eight weeks. I made the squad and was able to come back mostly, but my track sprinting days were over.

Fast-forward to my sophomore year where I was practicing in the field next to the entire varsity football team and marching band. I landed in a rivet in the grass and snapped my ACL. My claim to fame is that my screams stopped all practice, and maybe a few cars on the road. It took three football players to carry me to the trainer—two to hold my leg just so. I was told I would never run again, much less cheer and do gymnastics. But in six months, I was back in a brace like Akeem Olajuwon, notable UH and Rockets superstar, so I was cool. My nickname was RoboKate, after the ever popular *Robocop*. I had state-of-the-art fiberglass and metal. Some minor sprains and few setbacks, but all went well until the end of freshman year at Texas A&M. I learned to country swing dance, which is a lot like jive as it has lots of tricks, and my partner was knocked from behind while I was well above his head. That injury found me another surgery, during which I ended up getting a staph infection that required an eleven-day hospital stay, two more surgeries, three months of home care, and a year on oral antibiotics. I had to learn to walk again and I still have a minor limp. The staph ate all the repairs from surgery and I was the proud owner of a sixty-year-old knee at the ripe age of nineteen.

I calculated that I had spent nearly three years of my life on crutches and have had a total of six knee surgeries. At the last ultrasound, they told me I had a knee as bad as a ninety-year-old. I am due a knee replacement in my early forties. I had to give up any aspirations of athletic greatness and now I can't run or walk down stairs without holding on, or else my knee will give. I think this series of injuries to my knees is what defined me the most. Every time I wanted to feel sorry for myself, I would cross paths with someone who was worse off or had overcome more issues. I would have to dig inside and push. I think this is when I really began my analytic approach to people. I saw others who were going through worse and doing it. What were they doing? What could I learn and use? I believed if you studied books and people, you could solve most of your problems. I was in therapy with professional athletes and people who were just mowing their lawn, and I learned from all of them.

So, this led me to wonder how you ever know you've reached your potential. I think when you aspire to reach your potential, you are chasing a goal that is ever moving upward. If you reach it, do you then have more potential? This is a great motivator, and many great leaders have thrived and had successful outcomes, but I wonder if they thought they were successful, or great, or if they were still chasing their potential.

Thankfully, I didn't end up in a constant state of anxiety or on lifelong drugs to manage myself. Instead, I have studied people in situations and worked with many strategies to avoid being crippled by my own fear of failure or lack of perfection. This is not to judge people who take drugs to manage a situation, as sometimes that is the only option, but my history with drug allergies left me determined not to take medicine if I could avoid it, and has led to many nuggets of knowledge. I have spent my entire career working with others to achieve their potential. I started my career as a classroom teacher and for the last twenty years have worked with individuals to develop soft skills and become the best leaders they can in the business world.

Here is a glimpse into how I think each and every person can overcome mediocrity and achieve their desired goals.

Know Thyself

My first rule when I work with others is for them to "know thyself." I mean intimately know what makes you mad, what makes you sad, what brings you joy. If you don't like someone or you like someone else better, I challenge you to understand why— "just because" or "I don't know" does not work. You do know, is what I often say, you just can't explain it. So, work to explain it. What are your strengths? Everyone has strengths, or actions or activities, that come easier than others. In order to achieve and have continued success, you need to know yourself and be honest. It doesn't mean you can't accomplish something you are not good at, it just means you will have to have a strategy.

I once counseled a leader who, I believe, had absolutely no empathy. He had no capacity to understand the emotional state of others or himself. He was fair and extremely logical. In order for him to be a great leader, his employees needed to feel heard and not judged. When one of his employees told him they had cancer, he responded with, "Will you need to miss a lot of work?"

We actively began working on socially accepted conventions of the appearance of caring. I taught him that an appropriate response would be, "I am sorry to hear that, how can I help you?" What he really cared about was how work would be impacted. That's not to say he didn't care they had cancer,

I believe he did, but in his mind, he couldn't do anything about that, so he only focused on what he could do. This change in his question led to the information he felt was important and he learned appropriate responses. He really got to know himself and we used this to create an environment where employees felt heard. As a result, he did have success, at least by the engagement survey the next year where his employees felt their leader lead with empathy. This is not trickery, but a person understanding themselves and understanding how they can achieve the needed results.

I see the world as a bucket system, which I call my *Bucket Theory*. We have a bucket that represents energy and productivity. There are activities/ situations that fill your bucket, and activities/situations that drain your bucket. This is more tied to your internal drive, motivation and your overall mood. If you come home from work exhausted and with a low sense of accomplishment, look at your day, what you did. An entire day of back to back meetings where you get a lot of assignments to complete and can't start on any of them because there are more meetings—these days are "ocean boat" days. Ocean boat days are days when you feel like you are on an ocean in a small row boat. The task is doable but overwhelming. But I know back to back meeting days will make me feel overwhelmed, so I make sure that on those days I add activities/ situations that fill my bucket. For example, I may clean out an email folder, schedule lunch with my friends, or buy new office supplies. A new pen has saved me many times in my life! These may sound strange or silly to you, but I know they fill my bucket so I make sure I put them in bucket draining days.

Take a piece of paper and divide it into four equal parts. The titles of each section are:

1. My Strengths

2. My Not So Goods

3. Fills My Bucket

4. Drains My Bucket

You may add to and revise this list over several months, but it is critical to overcoming mediocrity and you will have more control over yourself.

Define the End State, or Ideal State

Now that you know thyself, you need to determine where you are going. Imagine the other side. Behaviors are a destination, just like Hawaii. Think about what you want to accomplish, and then really imagine the end state as if you could see it on Google Maps. What are you doing, why are you doing it and how do you know when you get there? Often, people will say they want to be a better public speaker. What is better? What do you do that you want to do better? As you keep asking yourself what, you start to analyze and define where you are going. If all you can say is *better*, then you most likely won't get there.

When working with a peer who hated presenting to audiences, I asked her why she hated speaking. She told me that she got really nervous and couldn't imagine that she had anything to share with the group as she wasn't an expert. Oddly enough, she was an expert in many areas, so her issue was a combination of skill and confidence. When I asked her to define the end state, she said she was up in the room discussing a topic without stuttering or using lots of "uhs" and "ahs." Additionally, she could answer questions and would welcome questions from the audience. So, we had the goal. I broke down the skill issues after observing her present to me in the comfort of her office and we simulated her presentations to develop expertise. I would ask questions to demonstrate to her the knowledge she did have on the topic. After several months, she began to find her comfort zone and develop her public speaking. She called me years later after she had just completed presenting to a room full of over a thousand people who were relegated to standing room only. She said, "I nailed it. I was confident, I never stuttered and I conveyed my passion and my topic to that entire room because it felt as easy as it was in my office with just you." The first step is determining where you want to go and creating a visual so real it is like a location on the map; you can see it, draw it and take a picture.

If You Need a Skill, GET It

As a teacher for over twenty years, I believe skills are learnable, and some are easier than others. With most business skills, you can learn it enough to become proficient. Use your strengths and your knowledge of yourself to obtain skills. In leadership development, I always say if you can't get it, hire it and surround yourself with people whose strengths are your weaknesses.

I hope these tricks will provide you with a path or at least an idea of the methods you can adopt to help you meet your goals and dreams. I believe all of life's events are opportunities to learn and determine a better way. I feel the smartest people are able to learn from those around them and not have to go through the pain for gain. If you see someone and you like how great they are at something, ask them their secret. Don't be afraid to explore and experiment.

Dr. Katherine "Katie" Waller

Dr. Katherine "Katie" Waller is a native Houstonian, and likes living near her childhood community where she is raising two daughters with her husband. She has many roles—dance mom, soccer mom, tutor, fanatic fan, pseudo-Uber driver, and guide on the side. She enjoys reading, dance, dry humor, and learning people's stories.

Dr. Waller is the owner and president of Vantage HRO, an HR consulting company in Houston. Over the last twenty years she has primarily focused on developing leaders and internal systems in a variety of industries. At Vantage, Dr. Waller and her team help clients create a people strategy that is aligned with their business strategy and goals. She believes that with people, you can achieve any business dream.

Dr. Waller has a doctorate in education in learning, design, and technology from the University of Houston. She recently completed her dissertation, focusing on strategies that teach interpersonal communication to leaders. Dr. Waller's background has a strong human resource specialty focus, centered around leadership development and coaching, organizational development, compensation, and process improvement. She has worked at several large organizations in Houston, including Compaq (a Fortune 500 company) and Texas Children's Hospital. She also served her hometown community as a classroom teacher specializing in math. She participates with local Texas A&M organizations to stay connected with the university from which she received her bachelor of science.

With Katie's passion for helping others and the enthusiastic spirit of her HR team, they continue to help companies achieve success on a daily basis. Her company works with all types of industries, including oil and gas, healthcare, accounting, homebuilders, and manufacturing companies.

Dr. Katherine "Katie" Waller
Vantage HRO
3611 Emerald Falls Drive
Houston, TX 77059
281-213-4919
katie@vantagehro.com
www.vantagehro.com

Barbara Beckley

The ROCK.. My Foundation.

What is Your ROCK in your life?

It was late one November evening when my mother came into my room and told me to sit down, she had something to tell me. "Your father is dead, he was murdered…"

R.O.C.K. – Foundation for Life

My father the Rock, not the wrestler or actor, but my father. I know everyone has their own feeling about their parents, but my father was the best, I called him my ROCK. He set a foundation for me that I continue to focus on day by day to get me through my life. My father was remarkable, open minded, caring, and kind (R.O.C.K).

John Beckley was tall, with a fair white complexion, a cool beard, and always made you feel like you were on top of the world. When I was five, he played Raggedy Ann and Barbie dolls with me. I loved playing school with all my dolls by being the teacher and my father brought it to life every time. Since I did not have any siblings, my father was my sister and brother. At age ten, he watched the *Wizard of Oz* with me seven times in one day! Every year he made me a homemade yellow cake with white icing for my birthday. He explained how a girl should be treated when I went on my first date.

He told me to dream big and believe in myself. My father graduated with honors and earned his bachelor's and master's degrees in business, but he always wanted to be a famous artist. That was his passion. My mother told him many times to just continue doing his regular management job, save money, and retire, but he loved to paint and draw. He did not stop his dreams and took on the challenges that came with the passion he loved. Any passion you are working towards takes determination and courage to deal with the good, bad, and ugly. My father wanted to make abstract art, which was not a favored genre in the art world as people were just starting to understand it. He believed this type of art should be respected and admired. Yet, he was often rejected by art shows. He worked very hard by changing his career focus and I learned from him that you can do what you set out to do, even if others do not believe in your passion or career choices.

As a white male married to a black woman with a biracial child, living in the seventies was difficult, but my father never saw color, he only saw the love he had for his wife and his daughter. This taught me to respect people and love them, not to judge a person by their color or background.

I was to dream *big,* and not doubt myself, to know that my daddy loved me, that he would always be there to protect me. He told me I was his angel and his hugs were magic. This was my ROCK in life.

Change of Events – Stepping Stone of the Rock

My life was forever changed in 1985 when my ROCK was smashed into tiny stones and blew away. I was seventeen when the call came late Tuesday evening, a few days before Thanksgiving. My mother picked up the phone and it was the police on the other end. The next thing I heard was my mother saying, "How am I going to tell my daughter?" I felt something cold come over me and knew something was not right. I could tell the pressure in my body was rising and suddenly I felt lonely and sad, but did not understand why.

My mother came to my room and told me to sit down, she needed to tell me something very important. I told her, "Just say it." Then the words came out, "Your father is dead. He was murdered in his apartment." She went on to explain the police found his body five days after he passed.

I couldn't swallow, I couldn't breathe. My mother went to get me some water; I immediately shut the door and locked it behind her. I tore up my room. Within a few minutes it looked like a tornado hit. My whole life had stopped, and I felt that every person in the world needed to stop to honor my ROCK that left my world.

My mother tried to unlock my door and her boyfriend had to knock it down in order to get me out and make sure I did not harm myself. Once my mother and the police made it in, I was in the corner balled up like a small snail, crying and repeating to myself, "I cannot live on, I cannot live on." My mother didn't know if I was losing my mind and could not even talk to me. The paramedics came and took me to the hospital. I was kept under observation for nearly four days. I just questioned what to do. It felt like my heart had been ripped out of my body. He did not die from a disease, an accident, or long-term sickness; he was murdered. Not given the choice to continue to live and be my ROCK.

I did not know how to handle this change in my life at the age of seventeen. I knew that the world felt very dark and lonely because my dad was gone forever. What was I supposed to do? I did not want to hear anyone's voice, or hear the words "I am sorry for your loss."

Why are you sorry, did you kill him? went my mind when I heard the same words expressed by family and friends as they tried to console me. But I was not in a frame of mind to be consoled; I just wanted to know why my father was taken away from me.

I faced three challenges: having to live without my father, my rock, dealing with my anger towards my mother, and figuring out who my father figure would be now. I had built up a wall with my mother because I blamed her for the situation my father had been in. If they hadn't divorced, perhaps he would still be here with me. I decided she was selfish to leave my father when he was trying to find his way in his art career that made him happy and excited to work every day. After their divorce, he was very unhappy and made some bad decisions when it came to another relationship that led up to his death.

Stepping Stone—Towards a Positive

The biggest change I had to make after my father passed away was to figure out my life goals and what I needed to do. Either I could just not care about my life and live in depression, not move forward in my education, career, or personal life, or I could use the death of my father to focus on becoming a straight A student, graduate from high school, and move right into college and build a career for myself.

We had the grim task of cleaning up his apartment. The smell of a decomposed body lingered in the air. As I looked at all the pictures my dad took of me and all the gifts that I found from past father's days and birthdays, I told myself I needed to honor my father in a positive way. He was murdered, but I didn't want his legacy to be murdered too, and that included me, his daughter.

I was his legacy—he taught and instilled morals in me, he worked with me on my homework assignments, and picked up books to help me study better for classes. When I was having problems, he always showed me how special I was and reminded me I could do anything I put my mind to. I knew I had to live the rest of my life making my father proud, to continue to grow, be an example, and the best I could be.

Have you had a loss or tragedy in your life? Do you feel helpless and abandoned? Do you ever wonder if you should just end it all and make it easier on yourself and others around you?

I am here to let you know that if you lost a loved one and they were your foundation and/or true love, you are not alone. You can move from the hurt and pain. Use the loss as an anchor, the foundation as your stepping stone to move forward in your life, and know that whomever you lost would want you to be the best individual you can be. It is not easy; in fact, you will have many days when it feels like the end of the world, but remember, you have a purpose and you have time to fulfill and search out your full potential within you. The pain and hurt of what you are feeling is your fuel and motivation to move forward and build yourself up.

According to the National Science Foundation, we average 50,000 to 70,000 thoughts a day, and seventy percent of them are negative. What I did to diminish some of my negative thoughts was listen to upbeat music, motivational books and tapes, and write in a journal when I felt sad, angry, and just about to give up. It was hard for me to find a close friend to talk to at the beginning when my father passed, so I relied on finding things to do to occupy my time. When I wanted to take my mind back to the fact that my father was gone and never coming back, I worked at being consistent in suppling my mind with things that were going to help me develop myself, because I chose to use my father's death as a foundation to honor him and believe in me.

In his book *Man's Search for Meaning,* psychiatrist and Holocaust survivor Viktor Frankl suggests that through traumatic experiences we search for new meaning in life; that we search for a reason to be happy despite the suffering. I told myself there was a reason why certain phases in my life happen and there is something to learn from them. I learned to turn the tragedy of my father's murder into a legacy, to let women and men know they can move forward and share how they struggled and worked towards being a better person despite what happened.

I had some hard times with relationships with men because I would look at them as a father figure instead of a boyfriend. That was a huge mistake because no one could take the place of my father, and it was not the boyfriend's job to be my father.

One boyfriend told me right to my face, "I am not your daddy, I am your man." That wake-up call was like a bomb in my head. That truly explained why my love life was not going in the right direction. I had put all the expectations from my father on to my boyfriend, and that was not fair to him or me. Others cannot fill a void in your life; you have to work on being whole for yourself in order to have a healthy relationship with anyone.

You must take the steps to move forward in your own life. You are putting a puzzle together, not putting a puzzle back together because the loved one you lost is not with you in human form. Use the lessons and advice your loved one gave you to build your new life while honoring them. What keeps me moving is telling myself my dad would be very happy with me when I do things right. And when I do things wrong or out of character, I say, "My dad did not teach me this," or, "I need to get a better understanding," because my dad would have told me to research the issue or problem at hand.

I continue to have a spiritual relationship with my dad. It gives me a sense of accountability and helps me deal with everyday problems in my life be it good or bad…you learn from both aspects.

Resolution

After the murder of my father, it took a lot of focus and energy to make sure I lived my life in a positive matter. I learned that I could not blame myself or my mother for his death; he made his own decisions and did not know someone would do something so cruel to him.

I had to tell myself I was not the cause of his death, nor was my mother. I had spent over ten years of my life just tolerating my mother, not wanting to be around her as part of me felt she had taken my father away from me. I was finally able to build a solid relationship with her before she passed away when I turned forty-five. My mother was a "tough" woman—she worked hard and did not let anyone take advantage of her or stop her from working towards her dreams. She was only four foot eleven, but very strong in her words. It took me to ask if I was destroying myself before forgiveness and communication finally happened. Once we talked everything out and I told her how I truly felt, she explained all the hurt she was dealing with and how she'd been blaming herself for years. We could not afford to have any more separation between us and we rebuilt our relationship.

I told myself I wanted to leave a legacy and pursue my education and career to make my father proud, which I have by obtaining two associate degrees a prosperous career in the insurance field for over 30 years. Now I am taking it to another level by telling my story so that others know they are not alone and can move forward after a huge loss in their lives. Your ROCK, foundation, the anchor that you had, can continue to be your motivation in your life. Their death does not have to cause death for you, because the person who passed away would want you to live on and shine, reaching others with your story.

I started a Women's Network Chapter in the Chicagoland area to help women come together to increase their knowledge and skills by learning and sharing their expertise with each other. I give each person who comes to the mastermind workshops a card that I created for them to keep as a reminder. The card has a picture of a diamond and says, *you have a diamond in you, just let it shine for others*. I tell this to all the ladies to remind them they have something special in them and they need to share it with others.

My story about my father, my ROCK, is something I will share anytime to make sure people know their tragedies don't have to be an obstacle, but can be the foundation to move forward and let that diamond shine. They can be a connection for others who need to see the light from the diamond. They will know there is hope, and they can move forward and succeed in what they want to do in life.

What talent, gift, or passion do you have in you that you want others to experience in their lives? Is there something stopping you from moving to the next level in your life? Are you holding any un-forgiveness in your life towards another person? Are you looking towards another person to fill a certain void in your life? I had to deal with all these questions one by one to make sure I was being true to myself and to make sure I was covering all bases in order to move forward and grow from the challenges I faced.

Whatever challenges you face in life, be it the death of a loved one, a certain place or memory that has been destroyed or replaced, the end of a career, or a breakup after a long relationship, dig deep, take all that negative energy and turn it into being a positive influence for others. When you focus on sharing and caring for others, you heal in the process. It took me talking about my father's death to not only connect with others, but to help me deal with the hurt and loneliness that I had not dealt with. I thought I was good and ready to move forward, but wasn't quite yet. The reality is its takes a person to be vulnerable and have courage to fight thought the pain instead of keeping it all inside. Don't let the hurt destroy you from being the person you can be. Don't be a prisoner in your own mind and body, take all that fuel and use it to guide you out of your own internal prison.

A rock is hard and heavy at times, sometimes small, sometimes large. It can hold down other objects, not move in a wind storm, and can sink to the bottom of an ocean and still keep the same look, shape and strength.

My ROCK might have been shattered, taken away from me, and might even feel like it's at the bottom of the ocean, nowhere in sight, but my ROCK is a steady reminder to me to continue to move forward in my life because he wants me to be the best. I know I have a diamond in me and I have to let it shine to help others.

Barbara Beckley

Insurance Expert/Professional Keynote Speaker/
Women's Group Chapter Leader

Barbara empowers women to overcome their challenges and helps them shine. Growing up in an interracial family in Chicagoland during the tumultuous 1970s imbued her with a bright inner light. This light has fueled her desire to help others. She believes people are people and that colors are there to remind us we all have filters to work through to appreciate the person underneath.

Knowing work and education were keys to success, she began working in insurance at age fifteen. Upon graduating high school, she obtained associates degrees in accounting and computerized business management, business management, and health administrative management. This landed her a job with AON Risk Services in their insurance department.

Wanting to become a better senior manager at AON, she found her true calling by joining a Toastmasters Club. Embracing the Toastmasters vision of improving communication and leadership skills, she worked her way up to becoming program quality director, providing educational opportunities for over 5500 Toastmaster's members. The great part is Barbara is just getting started. The beginning of 2017 saw her leading the first Chicagoland Chapter of the Women's Prosperity Network. Barbara's motto: "You have a DIAMOND in you." Let it shine because everyone has something special within them.

Barbara Beckley
Chicagoland Women's Prosperity Network
5615 73rd Street
Kenosha, WI 53142
262-344-1000
wpnchicago@gmail.com
www.womensprosperitynetwork.com/chicago/

Jeanne L. Lyons

A Whack on the Side of My Head

The delightful yeasty smell of baking bread was tantalizing my senses. I was in that dreamlike state between wakefulness and sleep, and with my eyes still closed I imagined slathering a still warm hunk with real butter. None of that fake margarine stuff for me! I awoke to see Joe sleeping next to me, his mouth half open and gentle puffs of breath exiting with each exhale. It was then I realized the yeasty smell was coming from him and not from baking bread. He had developed thrush, a mouth infection caused by the candida fungus, also known as yeast, and common to patients undergoing chemotherapy. I needed to call the oncologist before leaving for work. Thankfully, my scientific/medical training was being put to effective use doing end of life care for my fiancé, Joe.

Have you ever found yourself in a situation where you needed a number of whacks on the side of your head to get your attention? Don't feel bad. If you count the number of whacks I took, you'll find you are certainly not alone.

It was challenging holding down a job as world wide director of data project management for one of the world's largest contract research organizations. My travel schedule was increasing as the contracting company was adding the European data to their post market clinical trial database. The client could afford to be demanding. After all, this was the largest block buster drug of all time.

As I busily arranged to have a surrogate caregiver step in and pack for a whirlwind European business trip, six countries in nine days, I had the feeling the end would come very soon. Joe and I had this eerie connection where we could intuit what the other was thinking and feeling. He much more than I.

It seemed it was a trait I developed after meeting him. Getting on the plane heading to Scotland filled me with dread. I cried all the way across the Atlantic and tried to ignore the stares from the other travelers.

I met my woman-on-the-ground in Edinburgh and we had a strategy meeting over dinner to prepare for the client meeting the next morning. We knew this was going to be a challenge as both clients' representatives were high-strung New Yorkers. You know the type.

The most embarrassing times were in Madrid. It began when my client counterpart couldn't believe the cabbies didn't speak English. His Spanish was further shown to be lacking when he called the, surprising to him, female head of the Madrid office El Presidente. She looked down her nose at him and corrected with, "It's La Presidenta!" And it continued to deteriorate from there. From attending a brutal bull fight to trying to find somewhere to have dinner before 9:00 p.m., the stress kept increasing.

I could keep close tabs on Joe as I had the company provide me with an international cell phone, a novelty at the time. He seemed in good spirits and had me say "hello" and "goodbye" to him in the language of the current country. It was after another debacle of a meeting in Munich that I left for home. During a plane change in Switzerland I started to feel very sick. I kept trying to surreptitiously put my head down so the airline personnel wouldn't notice I was ill and deny me boarding. All I could think about was how I *had* to get home.

Twelve days later, Joe died peacefully in my arms.

If you know grief, you know it can be all consuming. I fought to keep my grief experience at bay. I still had two teenaged daughters, a household, and a high-pressure job to maintain. To add to the strain, my company fired my very supportive boss and replaced him with a new executive team. The political machinations escalated to a fever pitch as it became clear the "new broom" wanted to "sweep clean" and replace all the key existing players with ones of his own choosing. I became one of those who was sucked up by the vacuum of "progress."

This was too close on the heels of another similar incident a few years prior when I was promoted to acting director for a department in a prestigious and world-renowned teaching hospital. Politics, ego, and control led to my stepping back into my previous position as second in command. The new director, however, wanted a clean sweep. This was my first experience of having to leave a job not under my own volition. I was devastated! If I no longer held the position, then who was I? How would my family manage without the money I was bringing in? Who would put the roof over their heads and food in their bellies? Since I was still carrying benefits from the job, I felt the only way to provide for my family was for them to receive the death benefit from my life insurance.

I'm not sure exactly what I said to my counselor during my session, but I ran out the door to the safety of my car. Even though I don't remember the drive home, I do know I was thinking hard about how I could provide for my daughters. What could I, who was now nothing, give to my girls?

Shortly after my arrival home there was a knock on the door. When I answered, I was met by a sheriff's deputy. My counselor had called the authorities to report me as a danger to myself. That was one of the first whacks on the side of my head. Without a drop to drink, I sobered up fast. I was able to convince him I was no longer a danger to myself and avoided the mandatory seventy-two-hour hold in the county psychiatric ward.

I love my daughters with my entire being. I realized I was more than my job, I was a mother! How could I possibly leave them with such a legacy? How could I be so self-centered as to not realize how such an event would affect them?

During Joe's memorial service I met his aunt Bettina. We had a long and lovely talk and she invited me to visit her in her home in Carmel, California.

Bettina is a spiritual person. When we ate dinner that night she set a place at the table for Joe. It was during that visit she recommended the book

Many Lives, Many Masters by Dr. Brian Weiss. I readily identified with him as, with him being a medical doctor, our scientific training had similarities.

He at first doubted the past life phenomena. It was also a difficult idea for me to grasp. His book is so credible, however, and I was so desperate to believe, I wanted to learn more and more. After reading the book, I phoned Dr. Weiss's office in Florida and asked if he offered training in the past life regression technique. I was told he did, but usually only to professionals.

As I was busy traveling to interview for jobs in Texas and Southern California, I also explored the possibility of attending hypnotherapy school. I contacted one and was told their upcoming class was filled.

Driving back from the interview in Southern California, I was filled with anxiety. The highway was mesmerizing and allowed me to think about my choices. The headhunter told me I would receive job offers from both companies in the morning. What should I do? I just couldn't decide even though I was in a cold sweat from my uncharacteristic indecision. You know the drill. Find the pros then the cons and see which choice comes out ahead. Finally, I softly whispered, "Universe, I give it up to you."

The next morning, the phone rang and it was the headhunter. She was incredulous as she told me the Austin job decided to not fill the position and the San Diego job decided I wasn't a fit after all. Disappointed but relieved, I sat thinking about what to do next when the phone rang again. It was the hypnotherapy school informing me a student had dropped out of the upcoming class and there was a space available for me!

This was another awakening, or whack on the side of my head. By letting go of trying to control the situation, I could take advantage of this opportunity.

I loved the classes and all that I learned. It was also a very healing experience that brought me back to my center. It taught me to trust in something outside myself. Do you have to have empirical proof to make it true?

One of my profound and enlightening experiences with past life regression took place after a session I had with one of my teachers. While in trance, I was taken back to a time when I lived on a prairie. I am in a cabin looking out at the wind-blown grasses waiting for my husband to come home. As I turn back to look inside my house, I am filled with pride at the tidiness of it all. Everything is clean and neat and organized. Nothing out of place. Everything neatly put away.

Leaving my teacher's house and driving across the Golden Gate Bridge, I was enjoying the view of the ocean and feeling the warmth of the sun on my face when the realization struck me.

Another whack on the side of my head. The house and its contents were a metaphor! Back in the time of my prairie life there was neither time nor resources to make cupboards with doors or chests with drawers. Things were placed on shelves exposed to the eye and not hidden behind a covering. From this metaphor I learned everything I needed I had. It was in me. It is in you. All I had to do was open myself up to find whatever I was looking for. It was in my YOU-niverse!

Nearly one year to the day I began my studies to become a clinical hypnotherapist, I left for Florida to attend Dr. Weiss's class on past life regression and attain my certification in PLR. I was opened up to even more possibilities in my YOU-niverse and the power I have within. I was exposed to many other modalities and became an insatiable learner. I would have entertained none of this as valid just a few months earlier.

The field of energy psychology grabbed my attention when I was exposed to the Emotional Freedom Technique (EFT). I was a chocoholic. I don't mean that I occasionally binged on chocolate, I mean I could not go to sleep at night if chocolate was in the house. I became quite adept at knowing just how long to put frozen chocolate in the microwave so it became the gooey consistency I loved. Do you know what it's like having your children have to hide the Halloween candy from you?

While participating in a classroom EFT demonstration on chocolate cravings, I was the last person standing. It took about five rounds of the technique before I felt comfortable in handling my cravings. That was in August of 1999. In December of the same year, while reading the Christmas ads in the newspaper, I saw my favorite candy, chocolate turtles, on sale. I loved how when I ate them the nuts and the caramel would get stuck in my teeth so I could enjoy the flavors even longer. It was then I realized I had not had any chocolate since the classroom demonstration in August. To this day, more than eighteen years later, I still do not eat chocolate. What a powerful technique!

This led me on a quest to study more modalities in the energy field. From EFT, Be Set Free Fast (BSFF), and Time Line Therapy®, which I was privileged to learn from its founders, to Neuro-Linguistic Programming (NLP) and Mental and Emotional Release®. When I embark on a knowledge quest, I do not do it half-heartedly. I have become a certified trainer in NLP, Time Line Therapy® and hypnosis, as well as a certified Integrative NLP Coach.

So now what? What would you do with all this knowledge? I was back working at the hospital, which was always my fall back job. Even though I was well paid and had great benefits, I just wasn't feeling fulfilled. I felt the need to be able to use and share my new gifts and knowledge. I needed to find my purpose. As seasoned adults, do we really want to start something new? Live outside our comfort zone? Was it too late for me? I had been successful in the corporate world, but did I really have it in me to become an entrepreneur? How do I get started without the support of a staff? How am I going to make money?

A purposeful life does not need to be a single purpose. To quote a dear friend, "We did not come on this planet to pay bills." Just as I found I was not my job, neither am I the money I make. There are multiple purposes in our lives. If there were only one purpose in life, everyone would only have a single dimension. We are multi-dimensional beings. I needed to trust the universe that once I took the first step in my newly discovered purpose the money would follow. Once I realized it was time to move on, I knew it was time to change my life and my career.

I needed to take inventory of my life and what I had accomplished so far. I knew I wanted to expand my world by leaving mind-numbing work. Does it take a whack on the side of the head to find your life's purpose? Most people do not have the luxury of getting that whack in order to achieve professional/ life purpose. Or maybe they do, and they have just not recognized it. One can find purpose in nearly any kind of work. The purpose is in what it means to you and how you want to build upon it.

I have been lucky to receive multiple whacks and even luckier to have been able to recognize them—with help. One does not immediately flow from one experience to another. Some experiences need time to be processed, as in my prairie metaphor. Quite often we are so in to our "nose to the grindstone" mode we need help to build our awareness.

Being over fifty years old has its advantages. One is that you have a lot of transferable skills from multiple careers or jobs. It also means you have multiple experiences to look back upon and see the evolution of your purpose. Life and its purpose is very different for me with each decade I have lived until now and I hope to live in the future.

It began for me by taking inventory of what it is I could do well. The one thing I didn't do well was ask for help. Being the corporate executive and go-to person meant I needed to be the resource and have the answers. To become a novice again was difficult for me. To be honest, I believed that if I asked for help, people would think I was weak or incompetent.

Several years ago, I had a stroke following a surgery. This left me on a respirator, unable to talk or do anything for myself. I had to depend on my caregivers for everything large and small. Boy, was I angry! I was an independent professional woman used to making my own decisions! This was the type of situation where I had no choice but to ask for help. Again, another whack on the side of my head.

It was a valuable lesson to me that accepting help is not a sign of weakness. It was also an experience where, in allowing those whose purpose it is to be helpers, I could help them in fulfilling their purpose.

This was instrumental for me in pursuing my career in coaching. The program also gave me the opportunity to understand how coaching works. Coaching doesn't take away your independence, it enhances it. It helps you to recognize those whacks on the side of your head or jolts to the side of your heart that enable you to find your purpose and stimulate your forgotten dreams. It can help those people tired of the corporate nine to five world break out and become fulfilled. A good coach can show you a bigger picture for your life and invite you to embrace it.

We all have mountains and valleys in our lives and careers. Once we have reached a peak, if we stay there, it is no longer a peak. It ultimately leads to a valley. The key to moving on is in conquering our fears and having peak to peak experiences.

Very few of us know how many peaks and valleys we have yet ahead. If you are doubting your competence in going down new avenues, simply look back at other times you have faced obstacles and triumphed. Was it that killer sales presentation, the time you asked for a raise or promotion, or even when you took care of your sister's kids while she was on vacation? Remember, there is no failure, only feedback. Begin to walk down the road and then backfill what is needed and always know the YOU-niverse will support you.

Let me leave you with a quote from a woman who I greatly admire.

"It is very important that you only do what you love to do. You may be poor, you may go hungry, you may lose your car, you may have to move in to a shabby place to live, but you will totally live. And at the end of your days you will bless your life because you have done what you came here to do."

—Elisabeth Kübler-Ross

Jeanne L. Lyons

Fast tracking the business process enables you to get to the reason you became an entrepreneur in the first place. Conquering your fears, having peak to peak experiences, identifying your passions and realizing your own epiphanies without the pain of getting a whack on the side of the head is where Jeanne Lyons can help. Having walked the path of a mid-life career change herself, while being at the pinnacle of her field, will at least help her to soften any blows. She understands the gut-wrenching apprehension involved in the decision to become an entrepreneur.

The Accelerated Synergies™ programs are designed to quicken the learning curve in making a career change by breaking through the limiting beliefs of "I'm not good enough," "I'm too old," and "Do I really want to start over?" Jeanne's tools include techniques to alleviate the anxiety of leaving a comfortable and lucrative job, and her mastermind groups include educational components to establish an entrepreneurial business. These tools and programs will help to rapidly establish your entrepreneurial business and lessen the isolation and confusion which so often accompanies being a solo-preneur.

Ms. Lyons is an accomplished international speaker, coach, and author. Her broad Western medical training and more than thirty years of management experience with extensive regulatory and compliance knowledge gives her a unique perspective on holistic, energetic, and Eastern practices which complement her coaching.

She has a passion for the arts which feeds her soul. She has supported the community by being an ambassador for the chamber of commerce and an officer for various non-profit arts boards. She delights in helping others accelerate their success.

Contact Jeanne to receive Five Steps for Changing your Career.

Jeanne L. Lyons
Accelerated Synergies$^{(TM)}$
408-835-9950
lyo@earthlink.net
www.acceleratedsynergies.com

Michelle Kim

Let the Rocks Go: Release the Rocks that Prevent You from Seeing your True Potential

Have you been in a zone where you felt like life is full of possibilities? But then life throws painful rocks at us and we fall. We pick up these rocks and keep them in our backpack to remember why we fell. The rocks represent the injuries, failures, fears and doubts we experience. Despite all the challenges in life, we get back up, but life throws even more rocks at us and we fall again and again, picking up the rocks again and again. After a while, the backpack is too heavy to carry them all. Have you ever felt that way?

I remember the rocks that weighed me down every time I moved to a new place. Growing up, I attended five kindergartens, five elementary schools and three middle schools. That is thirteen schools, five countries, three continents! Every time I moved, I adjusted to a new school, learning a new language, and struggled with my education for a few months. As soon as I started making good grades, my mom, with her brown curly hair, would say, "미연아, 짐싸. 우리 이사가." "Miyon (Miyon is my Korean name), pack your bags. We are moving." Whenever I moved from one location to another, rocks were thrown onto my path and I tripped over them. Every time I fell, I picked up the rocks to remember why I fell. Many of these rocks had names like "unresolved grief" and "not belonging."

Every time I moved, I said goodbye to the home I had come to know, saying farewells to friends and the community I had become fond of. There were times when I did not find my place in the new community, but the interactions I'd made and the people I'd come to know had a place in my heart. Saying goodbye was like giving away a part of my heart. Each time my family and I moved, I went through an emotional funeral. I lost my friendships. I lost the comfort of conversing in my own language and the feeling of rootedness. The more I cherished the people and the relationships I formed, the more grief I felt. The rocks represented the unresolved grief. I was picking them up and filling my backpack with them. Over time, the grief had become heavier and heavier and I couldn't carry them in the backpack of my mind.

By the time I entered college, I was overwhelmed by the sadness of losses over the years but did not know quite how to put this emotional condition into words. I had not experienced many deaths of loved ones. Even though the losses I had were not physical deaths, proper burial and acknowledgement of the cherished people and the death of the world inside me did not happen and they were causing turmoil in my subconscious mind. At the same time, I felt this huge obligation to be grateful for the blessings from getting to live in so many countries at such a young age. Many of my friends said, "I am so jealous of you. You can speak three languages fluently!" "I wish I had traveled like you have!" While I agreed, deep in my heart I was hurt and lost. Silently, I was mourning for the world I had left behind that had evolved and moved on without me while I was too preoccupied with adjusting to a new world of reality that wasn't my own.

While unresolved grief was the first rock that weighed heavily on me, lack of belonging was the second one. I experienced extreme loneliness because I was not able to connect with people around me in a way that made me feel like I belonged. I tried every tool, strategy and technique to find my identity among peers but failed miserably and felt like a fish out of water. I could not fit in with the traditional definition of a Korean. I did not fit in with Asian Americans. I did not meet the definition of Japanese, New Zealander, American...although culturally I was influenced by each of these countries growing up. I felt most comfortable with people who did not have an expectation for me to be a certain way based on my genetic construct and background. The cross-cultural nature of interactions I had from childhood gave me many sets of values and norms to choose from and to live by. For example, between individualism and collectivity, I could choose to achieve personal success over the group's goals or choose to sacrifice my own desires for the whole. Between a guilt culture and a shame culture, I can choose between voicing my opinion based on my consciousness or giving subtle clues to others to save their face. Having many values and norms to choose from has caused me to feel like I belonged to many places—Universal—and was not limited to one. This meant that I was living in the margins of multiple cultures, not being able to feel fully secure in any one of them. For a long period of time, I wondered when I would ever feel at home with a tribe of my own.

When dealing with these rocks of unresolved grief and belonging issues, it was difficult to see beyond the current reality and see life as full of possibilities. Belongingness is in the middle of Maslow's hierarchy, right after the basic needs of food and safety. It is a psychological need that needs to be achieved before you can meet your esteem needs and self-actualization. When I was struggling, I Google searched for keywords related to the distressed conditions I was in and stumbled upon a website called TCKID.com. This is where I discovered for the first time a term called "third culture kid." This refers to someone who has spent a significant part of their developmental years outside their parents' home culture, having developed a unique "third" culture that is different from both their parents' culture and the local culture. While reading stories and comments written by many third culture kids on the website, I was crying over their pain as I had gone through similar experiences in life. Time after time, I saw patterns of similar stories and felt that something had to be done about this.

Having gained the vocabulary to describe my own experiences and the research that best described both the unique blessings and challenges of third culture kids, I wanted to give others a language to describe their own experiences and not feel alone. I became active in the online community, welcoming new members and showing my best form of compassion. I also founded a student organization on my college campus to raise awareness of the third culture kid issues. During the day when students could join different student organizations, I set up a booth to attract students who had similar backgrounds. I started coffee meetings for people to discuss their unique challenges and share their aspirations. I also invited Ruth Van Reken, the co-author of the Third Culture Kid book, as a guest speaker to provide hope and inspiration for the current generation. I am also privileged to have co-founded a nonprofit organization called MosaiK, which is dedicated to missionary kids that fall under the third culture kid umbrella. Since 2009, the organization has held an annual conference to provide a place for missionary kids to rejuvenate spiritually and receive support for their calling.

From my own journey of healing, I have come to know that it takes several steps to recover from unresolved grief. The first major step was acknowledging the gap between the past worlds and the current one. I became friendlier with my past by accepting it, reuniting the inner child from the past with the adult self. Then through deep introspection, I made a commitment to change myself by drawing on positive experiences from the past. Accepting my past and being more aware of my present has enabled me to create a bright future.

While I healed from the losses that took place, a sense of belonging was established through the journey. In order for you to achieve this, you must deliberately spend time with people who have the willingness to accept you for who you are without preconceived notions of how you are supposed to think or behave. It means surrounding yourself with people who are willing to meet you where you are instead of demanding or creating a world around themselves to feel safe in their own comfort zone. It's not limited to social status, religion, income-level and skin color. It comes from genuinely deep love and humility.

The rocks called unresolved grief and not finding a sense of belonging had weighed heavily on me. As I let go of these rocks in my backpack, releasing myself of the weight that I carried, I was able to see that life was full of possibilities. What are the rocks you carry in your backpack? What are some rocks that are preventing you from seeing your true potential? Don't you think it's time for each of us to go back and take those rocks out? Let us let go of these rocks so that you and I can be the men and women we were meant to be. Don't let those rocks take over!

If you'd like to learn about the characteristics of third culture kids and how to charter your journey of possibilities, you'll find a free gift at www.globalmichelle.com.

Michelle Kim

Motivational Speaker & Professional Keynote Speaker

Michelle Kim is a professional speaker who is fluent in Korean, Japanese and English. Drawing from her experience of having attended thirteen schools in five countries in three continents, Michelle speaks on the topics of emotional healing, resilience and self-fulfillment.

Michelle has juggled many rocks, including unresolved grief from repeatedly saying goodbye to loved ones, as well as not finding a sense of belonging in any culture but belonging everywhere at the same time. She carried these rocks in the backpack of mind for many years. Once she learned to let go of these rocks, Let the Rocks Go was born. Michelle uses this system to help her audience through keynote speeches and workshops to let go of their own rocks. Since 2008, Michelle has helped countless third culture kids find a sense of belonging. Michelle is passionate about using creativity to bring paradigm shifts. Every day she makes a new, extraordinary decision to help others become the men and women they were always meant to be.

Michelle Kim
Wheaton, IL 60187
847-665-9123
michelle@globalmichelle.com
www.globalmichelle.com

Sally Nauss

Aligning Your Life's Work to Your Life's Goals

Have you ever been so off course you wake up and realize you're exactly where you need to be? That's how I felt in 2009 when my world turned upside down.

Just three short years earlier, in 2006, I had the best job. I was getting paid to run in the some of the most beautiful cities in the world. From January to June, I ran in Paris, Malaga, Bangkok, London, Munich, and Orlando. I was lovin' it!

No, I wasn't a professional athlete, almost the polar opposite; I was working at McDonald's in the technology department. Our project was a global reporting system that would return rigor to standards that had become lax. Leading a team of dedicated IT professionals was challenging yet fulfilling.

When I wasn't working, I was training for an Ironman triathlon. The Ironman distance is 140.6 miles consisting of a 2.4-mile swim, a 112-mile bike ride, and a 26.2-mile run. I was registered for Ironman Wisconsin in September.

Ironman and my career were my focus and training and travel soon became my escape from the other parts of my life that weren't going so well, like my marriage.

A few months before my global travel schedule began, I was driving home from work and decided to call my husband to see if he wanted to go to Costco. He was depressed and I could think of nothing better to cheer him up than buying things we didn't need in bulk.

He didn't answer my call and I was in the garage by the time I was able to leave a message.

His car wasn't there.

"Hey, Tom, where are you? I was wondering if you'd like to go to Costco with me tonight. There're a few big things I could use your help carrying…"

I kept talking as I walked into the house.

"I know we haven't spent a lot of—hey, where are your guitars? Where are your shoes? I think we were robbed!"

Getting worried and not connecting the dots, I continued walking into our bedroom, still recording my voicemail.

"Your pillow's gone…did you move out? Oh my god! You moved out and didn't tell me. Where are you? What is going on?"

He had moved out and I had no idea where he was. So many emotions were going through me and I didn't know what to do first. I decided a locksmith would be my first call.

I had been so wrapped up in my career and training, I had lost sight of my marriage. Our daughter was going to school in England, studying abroad for a year, and I found myself living alone for the first time in my life. I went from my parents' house, to college roommates, back to my parents, and then to living with Tom. I had never had a chance to live alone and I was scared. Could I do it all alone?

My priorities shifted from focusing on furthering my career and the Ironman to seeing a counselor and trying to save our marriage. Training and travel gave me balance amidst the chaos of my relationship.

My husband was adamant I was the anchor weighing him down and not letting him soar to his dream of playing guitar in a famous rock band. He did play a pretty good rendition of *Henry the VIII* at my father's retirement home karaoke night. Was I holding him back?

Our daughter came home for Christmas and my husband moved back in for the holiday. We hadn't told her we weren't living together and decided to be a family for the week she was home. We both let out a collective sigh of relief when she went back to school and we could go back to our separate living situation.

By spring, I was tired; tired of traveling, tired of training, and tired of having my friends constantly ask about my marriage.

A trip to London in March was perfectly timed. It was an open-ended ticket—freedom for a few weeks and I would get to see my daughter. But by the second week, I was even tired of being away from home and my normal work and training schedule.

The hotel pool took only five strokes to cross and I didn't have access to a bike, but I did have my running shoes. Running gave me a chance to explore the neighborhoods, parks, and attractions of London without worrying about work and my relationship.

When my second weekend in London rolled around, I was exhausted and couldn't get out of bed. I don't know the last time I missed a Saturday morning run. Every time I thought I should be getting up, I fell right back to sleep. Finally, after the third call from housekeeping asking when they could clean the room, I forced myself to get up, walk to the closest restaurant— which happened to be McDonald's—and order dinner. I didn't have the energy to eat, and after only fifteen minutes I dragged myself back to the hotel to fall asleep again.

I took this as a sign I needed to get home and booked a flight for Monday afternoon. By the time I got to the airport, I could barely keep my eyes open. Sitting in the terminal, I fell asleep reading a magazine.

Fortunately, I woke up when they called my boarding group. I walked up to the gate agent and handed him my ticket. He asked if I was traveling alone and I confirmed I was. He proceeded to rip up my ticket right in front of me.

I froze. What was he doing? I needed to get home! I didn't have the will to ask questions, and just as I started to cry, he handed me a first-class ticket, saying, "It looks like you really need this."

Because of his kindness, I slept the entire way back to Chicago. I didn't know where this exhaustion was coming from but I needed to figure it out because I was training for an Ironman, had an important job, and was trying to repair my marriage.

Still going to counseling, Tom and I were learning to communicate better and he had moved back home. I had a conference in Thailand coming up and we decided he would join me after the trip for a much-needed vacation.

I still hadn't been able to shake the exhaustion and was falling asleep on trains, boats, and even the tuk-tuk rides—a tuk-tuk is a three-wheeled motorcycle with a cover. Like a Chicago cab, they weave in and out of traffic, go up on sidewalks, and don't pay attention to traffic signals. Even this lulled me to sleep. There was something wrong but I didn't have time to get it checked out. My intuition was screaming, "Take a break," but my ego was telling me "keep going and don't stop."

Once home, I only had one more trip to Orlando, then I would be home for the few months before the race. My coach and I mapped out my training plan for the summer. I would be working out at least two hours each weekday and four to six hours on the weekends.

My social life consisted of training. My friends were other triathletes. My co-workers knew I couldn't go to happy hours. I was boring to be around. Career and marriage took a backseat as I now had a single goal, finishing the Ironman. If I wasn't working, training, eating, or sleeping, I was planning my schedule. I didn't have time for anything else.

And then things changed.

Early on a Thursday, marriage-counseling day, I was on a twenty-five-mile ride before work. I got three miles from home and my calf started hurting. I got off my bike and stretched. It still hurt but I finished my ride. By the time

I got to our counseling appointment, my calf had swelled to twice its normal size. Keeping my leg elevated the rest of the day helped but it was still swollen the next day.

Weekends were big training opportunities, and that weekend I had an eighteen-mile run and a 110-mile bike ride planned. Because of my leg, I cut my run to eight miles and the bike to eighty. I realize now how crazy that sounds, but at the time, it seemed completely normal.

By Tuesday, I could barely walk, and the trip from the parking lot to my desk at work was excruciating. When I got to my desk, I put my head in my hands and started to cry. Not one to show emotion, especially at work, I tried to regain my composure quickly. A co-worker had noticed me limp in and cry at my desk. She came over and handed me a piece of paper with two doctors' phone numbers and said if I didn't have an appointment with one of them in thirty minutes, she was going to call an ambulance.

I called, made an appointment with one of the doctors, and was in his office before noon. He was young and used to dealing with athletes. Because of my general good health, he didn't think it was anything serious but sent me to the hospital for tests.

I had an ultrasound on my leg and the technician wouldn't tell me anything. The test took forever and all I wanted to do was find out what was wrong and go back to work. When they were finally done, they told me to sit in the waiting room while they sent the results to the doctor. As I was waiting, the phone next to me rang and the receptionist told me to pick it up, the call was for me.

They found a blood clot and I needed to get on blood thinners as soon as possible. They put me in a wheelchair and admitted me to the hospital.

Here I was, the healthiest person I knew, and I was in the hospital learning to give myself injections of blood thinner in the stomach.

The realization I wouldn't be able to do my Ironman hit pretty quickly.

After I was released from the hospital, I couldn't do anything for a week as I was on complete bed rest.

Training had been my life and I didn't know how to handle the down time. By the time I was able to return to work, I was bored, and instead of taking a step back and re-evaluating, I applied for and got a job with more responsibility and more travel. I needed to stay busy and have something to do with my time.

The reason I got a blood clot was a genetic factor. I don't know why it took over forty years to manifest or why it happened during a very stressful time in my life, but I wanted to find out. All the time I had been spending on training was channeled into researching how to get off the blood thinners and prevent another blood clot.

I heard about Eastern Medicine and started researching the effects of diet on health. I consulted with doctors and read everything I could get my hands on. I read *The China Study* about the effects of the standard American diet (SAD) on health and it seemed like all signs were pointing me toward a plant-based diet. I went vegan cold turkey the week of Thanksgiving. I was now vegan working at McDonald's.

My co-workers had been used to my training schedule but now they had to figure out my eating. Working at McDonald's with someone who couldn't eat from the menu was confusing. How to handle team lunches and dinners? Steakhouses were the favorite go-to restaurants while traveling and I would order a baked potato and broccoli. Staying healthy was my motivation.

The idea of an Ironman was still in the back of my mind but I didn't know if I'd ever be able to train for and finish one. I had cheered on my training partners that summer, watching them reach their goals of becoming an Ironman, but for me the goal seemed more elusive than ever.

When a friend called me and told me Ironman Arizona switched their dates and spots were available for the next year, I registered and training began again. This time I decided to coach myself because at the time, I didn't know any coaches supporting a plant-based diet. It seems like a long time ago because now there are books, websites, cookbooks, and coaches that cater specifically to vegan endurance athletes.

My job took me to Arizona several times before the race and I was able to train on the bike and run courses. I was grateful for each training session accomplished and felt very lucky to have the support of my family, friends, and coworkers. My decision to eat a plant-based diet helped me get off the blood thinners within a year. I was healthy, felt good, and was confident I would finish the race.

The day of the Ironman was the day of our nineteenth wedding anniversary. Much like my wedding day, every detail of the day was planned out. I had outfits for each part of the race and all included black lycra, were comfortable, and certainly not flattering. I knew what I would eat when—a Payday bar at mile eighty on the bike, and pretzels and Coke during the run— and what mile someone would hand me a glow stick to wear around my neck so I could be seen in the dark.

At the swim start, treading water, I was bubbling over with anticipation, wondering what the day would bring. I looked up and spotted my cheering section, my husband, my daughter, and a friend, on a bridge above me. Just seeing them and knowing they were there calmed me down.

The day couldn't have been more perfect.

I finished the Ironman in fourteen hours—the goal I set for myself.

I was an Ironman.

Reaching a goal is sometimes anticlimactic. You plan and train and visualize and then the day comes and goes and you're left with your memories of the event. Not once in my training did I think about who and what I would be after I finished the Ironman. My visualization had stopped after I heard the words, "You are an Ironman."

Back to my regular routine, something inside shifted and I realized I had a new perspective. What I had trained for and accomplished changed who I was and gave me new insight on who I could become. I was excited to help others pursue their dream of completing a triathlon. I was also excited about how much energy I had eating a plant-based diet and I wanted to talk to and learn from others eating this way.

I saw another path that didn't include the stress of my career and relationship. I was afraid of the unknown but knew I could handle the decisions I needed to make.

It took me a while to realize my extreme exhaustion came from being so far out of alignment with my values. I was working too hard at being someone I thought I should be, running from appointment to meeting, I didn't stop to see my strength was running.

The year after I finished the Ironman, my husband and I divorced. I left the career I had worked so hard for at McDonald's and started a business coaching triathletes. My business has evolved and expanded over the years focusing on coaching business owners to have healthy businesses and healthy bodies.

I am still working on the big life lessons of love and forgiveness but some of the lessons I've learned in my pursuit of a life well lived are:

Follow your intuition. After I was given a chance to be still and listen, I didn't see it as a gift and instead took on more responsibility. Running is my outlet to clear my mind and work through perceived problems but when I couldn't run, I didn't know how to stop thinking about the past and worrying about the future. I've since started meditating – it wasn't easy – but on days I don't run or when I need to take a break from a problem, it helps me clear my mind. I started by taking 5 minutes to close my eyes and breathe. I'm not ready to spend time at an Ashram but I notice my mind doesn't race as much and often I find the next right step.

Set goals aligned with your values. Setting goals and tracking where I am in achieving them is how I stay focused and on track. But I've learned to set goals aligned with who I am instead of whom other people tell me I should be. I don't immediately say yes to every great opportunity. My response has become, "Sounds interesting, let me think about it." And once I make a decision, I don't ruminate about it, I dive in or move on.

Just do it. Many of the women I've coached have big dreams but they don't act on them because of fear. We sabotage our lives with our thoughts and fears but all we need to do is take one step to get to the finish line or decide it's not for us. We play small and stay in the box we created for ourselves because we are afraid of who or what we will become if we try something new. We don't want to hurt anyone's feelings or shake up the status quo so we don't even try. One of my favorite quotes by runner and author John Bingham is "The miracle is not the I finished, the miracle is that I had the courage to start." Unless we take the first step, we don't know where our path will lead us.

We can't change the past. Ironically the job I left at McDonald's was Senior Director of Alignment. I was aligning the goals of the company but not my own. In the end, it's clear there were no wrong turns or wasted miles only life's classrooms. Ultimately alignment with values and goals is personal and can't be measured by a 5K time or a balance sheet. Today it's not a title I am chasing; my work comes from the inside out in integrity with who I am.

Sally Nauss

Sally Nauss is a role model for creating a business in alignment with your values. Sally left a corporate job in 2010 (she was a vegan working at the Golden Arches!) to pursue a career in fitness. She later founded Active Souls, an award-winning women's only fitness center.

Building her company with her corporate background, Sally learned powerful lessons about the importance of systems and how all the elements of leadership, operations, finance, team building, marketing, and sales fit together to create a business that can run independently of the owner. She closed the doors of her fitness center and now coaches small business owners on systems and accountability for growing their business and creating the lifestyle they desire.

An avid runner and triathlete, she is passionate about sharing the positive effects of a balanced diet and exercise program have on overall health and energy. She is certified in life coaching and behavior change and uses this experience to help business owners create positive results.

Sally works with highly motivated business owners who want to grow their profits and have a life filled with energy, passion, and abundance. She offers one-on-one, group, and online coaching.

Sally Nauss
SAN Coaching
La Grange, IL
630-235-3673
sally@SANCoaching.com
www.SANCoaching.com

Melissa McSherry

The Tiny Word That Revolutionized My Life

The email came in just after eleven in the morning. My client needed a "tiny" thing done that would throw off my entire day and have me stressing to do everything I'd already committed to.

Couldn't I just do this one little thing? I'll move this other thing over and skip lunch, I thought. By now, I was pretty good at these mental gymnastics.

But for whatever reason, on that day, a new thought occurred to me. Was this really an emergency? Couldn't it wait? Without much thought, I wrote my client back and explained to him why it didn't work for me. I hit send.

And then I freaked out.

He was going to be outraged, I was certain of it. He would realize I was unreliable and look for someone who was able to come through.

To my utter shock, he wrote back and said he understood.

"Has it always been this easy?" I said aloud. *Yes,* yes it has been.

I had spent my life fighting these silent battles in my head, but this martyr mindset was doing nothing but creating a life that was way harder than it had to be. My life at the time was out of control, with endless running around. I was just starting out as a business coach, but I was close to burning out—and I'd barely had any clients yet. But by putting so many other people first, the only thing I was building was debt, a horrible attitude, and a ton of stress.

Why was I not seeing any success for myself when I was so busy? My mile-long to-do list was actually a massive procrastination device—one that kept me from having the time to go for my dreams. The scary ones. The ones that mattered.

I could never have predicted how that morning's little email exchange, me timidly standing up for myself, my sanity, my happiness, and my own priorities, would be the catalyst for my divorce.

This may sound overly dramatic, but hear me out. Up to this point, I didn't even realize there was a choice to be made.

In my twenties, I got married and later had a son, and was on the path to be a full-time mom with a house full of kids. I was content with that trajectory—until my husband told me he didn't want a second child. In that split second, I realized I was staring down *a lot* more free time than I had planned.

Naturally, I started wondering, *What else am I going to do? How do I want to spend my time? And with whom?* So, I started dabbling in self-help and various forms of personal development. What I came to realize was that my life was already pretty good.

And that was the problem. It was good. It wasn't *great*.

My husband, although loving, didn't push me in the ways I needed. Sure, he was kind and wanted to make sure I was comfortable. And sure, comfort felt nice, but nice—as I was coming to understand—was for pushovers, not badass business owners like I wanted to be. I wanted *more* than a predictable life, so I asked for it. I asked for a divorce.

That night, as I put our son to bed, I kissed him as I rocked him and silently cried over I was about to do. I managed to tell my husband that I wanted a divorce in between sobs. He was amazing. At the end of the conversation, we hugged each other and he said, "I will always love you." And I said, "I will always love you, too."

This is not to say that if you start to improve yourself you'll end up ending your marriage. It just happened to be the case that when I dug deep, I saw that I had so many options.

I realized that I wasn't happy in my marriage, and it was more than what we could work through in couples' counseling. There was something else out there for me, even though I didn't know what it was just yet.

After the divorce, I started saying no to other things, too. No to overworking. No to getting by on four hours of sleep—which used to be my badge of honor. No to playing small, getting walked on. No to letting life just happen to me.

By learning how to say no, I then had to learn how to really say yes. If I was going to do this, really do this, build a life on my terms, start my dream business, and go for extreme happiness above all else, I'd have to relearn when to say yes.

So, I started saying yes strategically. I said yes to a grocery store delivery service so I could have more time with my son and I hired a housekeeper once a month—a big deal at the time since I was now a single mom and money was tight.

Instead of saying yes to get-togethers with friends who were only interested in towing the line, I started saying yes to networking meetings where women business owners hung out. Such meetings are full of strong, ambitious, and successful women because smart business owners know that surrounding yourself with other smart business owners is key.

Even though I was nervous, I would go to these events, scan the room, and pick out three women who oozed success and confidence. Then I'd invite them to coffee.

Two things happened: I spent less time with people who drained me or didn't understand that I wanted more than just getting by. And I started making important business connections, women who referred me to potential clients and who believed in me until I could see the truth for myself.

These new relationships fueled me. I realized that I needed to continue surrounding myself with people who didn't want to just stroke my ego, listen to me whine, and let me get away with good enough. I needed someone to hold me accountable and give me action steps. So, once again, I did what had previously seemed impossible because of money and my self-imposed limitation that I had to do it all on my own, and I hired a business coach.

The first thing she taught me was how to pick and choose what got done.

When I first heard my coach say that there should only be three things on my to-do list, it felt like she broke my brain! But when she showed me how to swap my priorities, I actually got more things done, and more important things.

Suddenly, I had more time, and as a result, my business started profiting. In three months, I was able to double my income. This meant I could keep doing things that would allow me to grow my business, and in turn, help me help more people, have greater joy and purpose, and actually have better quality time with my son. Today, my quality of life is higher than I ever imagined.

I've always been extremely independent. I prided myself on being the girl who moved to Seattle by herself to go to theater school, on being a single mom whose son is on the autism spectrum. When you say those things out loud, people think you're a rock star. That charade of being Ms. Independent was my personal validation, but it was killing me. I thought I was powerful, and I was, but I was wasting my power in the wrong places.

The old me would go to business conferences under the guise that I was doing something good for myself. But I would get home, never take action, and quickly return to my favorite form of self-sabotaging—overextending myself. But now that I was trying to start a new business that was all mine, I needed to figure out how to do it so I wouldn't stay stuck in a victim mentality, thinking, *Oh, I'm just a single mom, so of course I won't be able to pull it off.*

The first step was to get clear on what I wanted. First up: I needed a sane schedule that didn't lead to burnout. Now that I knew what I wanted, I could figure out how much time I had in my day to work on my business, and which ways could I maximize that time.

One of the keys was learning how to focus on profit-producing avenues. If I mastered this, then I would have a smaller to-do list and more revenue. I'd get the important things done, let others slide, and be more fulfilled at the end of the day.

Ever since I learned that skill, the women I've coached have caught on quicker than I did. I would teach them what I spent five long years learning the hard way, and they would see results in a month. They figured out what was truly important and defined success on their terms—whether that's making more money in one month than they once made in a whole year, having a schedule that allowed them to pick their kids up from school every day, or starting a business that ignited positive change in the world. It's a beautiful thing to witness women shorten the learning curve and create the lives they want.

Yes, you *can* have it all. You can have a happy relationship, family, career, and business. I'm living proof that once you start to say yes to the things that matter most—and no to other things that don't bring joy—life becomes unrecognizably beautiful.

Melissa McSherry

Melissa McSherry has been a successful entrepreneur since 2010. She has launched two successful businesses, doubled her monthly income, and created a true life by design, all while raising a six-year-old son. She has worked with hundreds of entrepreneurs, helping them slash their stress while doubling their income, doubling their free time, and creating everything they want out of their business and their life.

Melissa McSherry
Better Than Before
1507 W. Victoria St. #1
Chicago, IL 60660
303-895-5866

mel.mcsherrycarr@gmail.com
www.melissamcsherry.net

Sharmila Wijeyakumar

A Journey to Freedom: Overcoming Modern Day Slavery

Waking in a cold sweat as flashbacks of rape shuddered through me, I couldn't deny the small, still voice that accompanied the memories, whispering, *You can help them.*

As disturbing as the flashbacks were, it was the voice that terrified me. No stranger, the voice had come many times before in the night, and I had chosen to ignore it. The more persistent it was, the more I wanted to run from its directive. I turned over, praying, knowing only God could remove the fear but also knowing that I evaded His calling. *Not now, Lord, I can't. It's too hard!* I silently entreated. *Ask someone else, I'm not the right person. I'm broken. Afraid. Not good enough.*

These little talks with God began to happen more regularly. I would hear Him reassure me, *You can do it. I am here with you.* Not audibly, but in a whisper in the quiet of my mind during Bible study.

Drawn to Luke 4:18 and Isaiah 61:1, I read, "The Spirit of the Lord is on me, because he has anointed me to proclaim good news to the poor. He has sent me to proclaim freedom for the prisoners and recovery of sight for the blind, to set the oppressed free." As a survivor of human trafficking, the mandate was clear: set these people free—the victims, the oppressed; johns, the blind who didn't know what they really purchased; and pimps, prisoners beholden to organized crime and drug bosses, who also needed to be freed.

Reading Moses' story, I saw that he too felt he was not good enough. Every woman in the Bible who changed the course of history had been abused or neglected in some way. I realized that, while I may feel broken and imperfect, God can still use me if I abide in Him and obey His will. After all, Noah built the ark during a drought and everyone ridiculed him. I figured, since Noah was obedient, and God brought rain in His timing, I could trust Him and see what happened if I took steps forward.

I was blessed at the time to be employed by a tech start-up that encouraged us to try new applications with the software we produced. I developed a business intelligence project in my spare time, using predictive analytics to pinpoint trafficking hotspots in the UK, Europe, Africa and South America. At first, I worked completely behind the scenes, not even telling my husband or family. Fear filled me, as I had yet to learn to trust God or others again. Being misused by people had taken its toll. I was wary of people's true intentions, still unable to forgive myself for my past, or anyone who had a hand in the making of those experiences. I still sought God's healing.

Forgiveness was one of the hardest concepts I battled to accept on my journey to freedom from modern-day slavery. Used and abused by countless men, I will never know most of their names, and their faces blur in my memory. A few stand out, although they represent *symptoms* of the problem, not the cause of the problem itself.

I was first trafficked when I was a teenager. Conned into believing that I was being hired as a nightclub hostess, I ended up trapped in a brothel. I've always been a fighter, so resisting came naturally to me—not the kind where you punch people, but the kind where you tap an inner drive to solve problems.

Traffickers *want* to break you down—spiritually, physically and emotionally—so that you rely on them, instead of God or yourself, for *everything*. They decide when you eat, use the phone, use the bathroom, sleep and work, servicing men.

Coercion is the trafficker's favorite tool. It takes many forms, the most common of which is isolation. Traffickers separate you from family and any social network or support in every area of your life. The isolation may be outright physical or the result of emotional manipulation. The more isolated you are, the lonelier you feel and the less anyone can coax you down any other path but the one the trafficker presents. If everyone around you is also trafficked, and all you hear is how pretty you are, beauty comes to carry a hefty price. You come to believe you are worthless and your beauty only makes you vulnerable to abuse.

People wonder how this downward spiral is possible, but—especially if you already feel like a disappointment—believing bad stuff about yourself can often be easier than believing the good stuff. Repeated trauma changes you, so that you believe you deserve to be hurt, and that pain is normal. *People in pain like that can only hurt other people.*

Forgiving one's trafficker—someone who took every inch of your life, broke you down and molded you into what they wanted—comes at a cost. Forgiveness requires *letting bitterness go*. Bitterness is the warm, comfy blanket that trafficking victims often wrap themselves in as a defense mechanism against the world. It comes with matching blankets of shame and insecurity caused by an inability to trust. To put down these blankets took years of therapy and a deeper understanding of who I am in God. To this day, if I were to step away from God's grace and mercy, those defenses would be easy for me to arm myself with again.

Bitterness caused me to decide poorly and reject genuine opportunities because I didn't trust myself or those around me. Thank God my Uncle Ranjit and his wife, Aru Aunty, my other Aunt (Periamma) and Grandmother (Ammama) patiently helped me to understand that I was the apple of God's eye. Along with my pastor and our local church, they helped me to see what unconditional love looks like in human form. I made it hard to love me at the time. It takes special people to overlook self-destructive behavior and choose to love the person anyway. I wanted to build a compassionate community like that myself, but I still clung to the "safety" of my insecurity blanket.

Enter Rev. Dr. Denardo Ramos, my husband of twenty years as this book goes to print. A graduate of seminary with a PhD in human services, he understood how to help me heal, while calling me his "Capitamonte," his porcelain doll, made in Sri Lanka—I'm Sri Lankan by ancestry though not born there. Denardo accepted me, warts and all. Starting our family helped me understand God's love for us as His children. For the first time, I could love unconditionally and felt loved. I experienced the loss of a child when my first tumor was discovered and triggered a miscarriage. I now had tools to move forward in love and the knowledge that "all things work together for the good of those who love the Lord and are called according to His purpose." (Romans 8:28)

The voice of God continued propelling me forward, urging me to start a program to save other women trapped in a life of human trafficking, but I was still unsure that I was capable. However, I had developed a lucrative career in software with a niche competency in launching software into new markets. This newfound stability gave me the space to take a risk.

Prayer guided me to join a European project to stop child trafficking in thirteen Spanish-speaking countries, where I could serve while keeping my day job. I traveled extensively for work, seeing firsthand the lengths people will go to obtain special services from virgins or young boys or girls. I learned how affluence in the wrong hands contributes to the demand for trafficked children. According to International Labor Organization (ILO) figures, commercial sexual exploitation accounts for $99 billion of a $150+ billion global human trafficking industry, while some put numbers closer to $1 trillion worldwide.

While in Europe in 2006, I read *Rediscovering Church* by Bill Hybels and understood that the community structure described could aid survivors' recovery. I tucked this idea away, and didn't think of it again for years because I could not imagine that such a place existed. The community does exist, in fact, in churches around the world. "The local church is the hope of the world,"

Hybel writes, and they are critical in the fight to stop human trafficking.

We spent the next six years in Europe, continuing to battle slavery. Trafficked victims are used for unpaid labor, sex and as drug mules—and sometimes, simultaneously for all three. We witnessed chilling atrocities, like the insertion of heroin instead of silicone into breast implants to transport the drug. Women often died after the transaction, but if they survived, they were sold into prostitution, their implants replaced by silicone. We have seen countless girls shoved full of drugs and boys forced to swallow them, to be driven back and forth across borders as drug mules. The ILO has determined that human trafficking is the third most profitable crime after illicit drug and arms trafficking, which often, as we have seen, involves human trafficking victims as well.

You may think that this only happens overseas, but the US is considered the world's major destination for human trafficking, per a University of Illinois study. The average age of entry into prostitution in the US is twelve for a girl and eleven for a boy. The UN defines any underage sex trade as coercive, and therefore trafficking. Children of this age don't willingly choose prostitution; it is forced upon them by circumstances or torture.

In 2012, my family and I returned from Europe. We felt God was calling us home, and we wanted our daughter to have an American college experience, ideally at my alma mater, Purdue University in Indiana. We moved to Illinois, and decided to take a little break from serving while we sought God for next steps. By accident—or Divine design—I drove past Willow Creek Community Church and immediately had the epiphany that *this* was the church with the community model I had read about all those years ago. Intrigued, we visited and decided it was a great place for our family to hide in the pews...but God had other plans for us.

In the meantime, I found an amazing job that I love with Liferay, an enterprise software company based around Christ-centered leadership with a firm commitment to work-life balance. Their supportive culture has blessed me ever since.

Our lives took another surprise twist when Denardo and I were put on part-time pastoral staff at Willow Creek Community Church. Leading 1,500 singles across three services, it was through Section Leader coaching by the Willow team that I garnered the courage to finally start telling my story publicly. I discovered that I could mobilize people to fight trafficking. This newfound impact coupled with my own survivorship compelled me to establish a nonprofit organization with my husband. Rahab's Daughters is a ministry that rescues, rehabilitates and reintegrates victims of modern-day slavery by guiding them down a path of physical, emotional and spiritual healing.

Make no mistake, slavery is exactly what it is. Today, there are more slaves in the world than there were before we abolished slavery and we are losing the battle, with another person falling victim to trafficking every thirty seconds.

Many have told me that fighting human trafficking is a hopeless effort, that we can't accomplish such a big change, but I am encouraged by history. William Wilberforce was but a solitary man who rallied for the abolishment of slavery in the late 1700s. As Rahab's Daughters and other organizations work to raise awareness, I believe that just as in the past, people will rise up and put greed aside to free slaves and end the demand for trafficking. We have the power to end modern day slavery, together.

Sharmila Wijeyakumar

A wife and mother, Sharmila Wijeyakumar enjoys serving others, traveling and spending time with friends and family. She has a bachelor's degree in interpersonal and organizational communication from Purdue University, with minors in psychology and management information systems. A senior account executive at Liferay, Sharmila has a long and distinguished career in enterprise software sales, with a specialization in new market launches. She has been honored in the Who's Who of Professional Women in IT. A published author, she enjoys helping tech start-ups. Whilst pursuing her software career, she dedicated her life to God, and to ending human trafficking, including work globally to reduce the number of child trafficking victims in thirteen Spanish-speaking countries. Sharmila is widely recognized as COO and co-founder of Rahab's Daughters, a nonprofit organization that rescues, rehabilitates and reintegrates victims of human trafficking. Selected as one of CRN magazine's

Women of the Channel four years in a row (2010-2014), the Daily Ledger also named her one of the most Influential Women in Suburban Chicago. In 2017, she won a Stevie award for Female Executive of the Year. Sharmila spreads joy and compassion wherever she goes.

Sharmila Wijeyakumar
Rahab's Daughters
18-5 Dundee Ave #200
Barrington, IL 60010
260-460-0492
samw@rahabsdaughters.org
www.rahabsdaughters.org

Sharon M. Wilson

The Stepmom Journey: Get to Know YOU First

In 2009, as I approached my fortieth birthday, I was increasingly holding grudges. I felt I was the only one making compromises in my marriage, was feeling left out by my blended family, and was irritated that my intentions were often questioned. I was a mental mess and the relationships most impacted were those with my husband, my seven-year-old daughter, and my twenty-two- and twenty-eight-year-old stepdaughters. In my eyes, those relationships were broken because mentally, physically, and spiritually, I felt broken. Thoughts of giving up and getting out of my marriage were coming far too often. I felt like a fraud; I was outwardly appearing to have it all together, yet I felt completely out of control.

I understand now that our relationships with others are a direct reflection of our relationship with ourselves. It is very likely that if we are insecure, we are judgmental or defensive; if we are hurting, we are likely hurting others; if we are unhappy, we likely notice and point out faults of others. Just having this awareness earlier on in life would have provided me a valuable opportunity to approach my role as a stepmom in a more realistic and positive way. I did not have strong enough self-awareness to understand how my beliefs and past shaped how I treated others, nor the awareness of how others' struggles defined their behavior towards me.

The Choice to Become a Stepmom

In 1999, as I married my husband, I had no idea the impact that choice was going to have on who I am today. In the beginning, the idea of being a stepmom did not faze me; in fact, I was excited as I felt it would give my life more meaning and purpose.

When I met my stepdaughters at the ages of ten and sixteen, all was good. My husband was completely up front early on, sharing that both of his girls had separate moms from two different marriages, and each daughter also had another sibling. His intention was to do whatever it took to keep his girls close. While a bit shocked by the complexity, after having gone through my own recent divorce, I had let go of the idea of a "perfect" relationship. I knew these relationships would take time for me to build, but for the most part, I felt we got off to a good start. We were going to be an instant family, and I was just going to be an extra person to love them. I wasn't completely naïve as I knew it would be complicated, but if we had good intentions and I did not plan to get in the way, it would all work out, right?

Wrong. For most stepparents, "getting in the way" is a constant feeling. In fact, you "get in the way" even before you say "I do," just as a *potential* stepparent. To be a stepparent, you need a strong sense of self. Looking back, I was insecure. I cared what others thought of me, I wanted to be liked, and I was a people pleaser. As a result, I took so much personally in my role as a stepmom. I did not always consider what was behind those behaviors and encounters within the blended family: kids' life experience, their emotions, their parents' relationship, their parents' emotions.

Parenting is already complicated, so when you add in an extra layer of past marriage(s), kids, and exes to the mix, the role of a stepparent becomes even more complex. You see, there is no such thing as "the role of a stepparent," as it is extremely unclear and dependent upon all that is underlying. As a parent, our goal may be to raise healthy, smart, responsible, happy, and educated kids. So, then, what might be the role of a stepparent in raising those same kids, in terms of their health, discipline, happiness, and education? If you polled ten different blended families, you would receive ten different answers.

I just had no idea what a unique role being a stepmom was going to be and had little time to figure it out.

Balancing the New Stepmom Role and Marriage

Immediately upon becoming a stepmom, our new family experienced a decade of life events that we were not prepared for and that significantly impacted our marriage. It was one after another as we started our new family: several untimely deaths, including my husband's brother and my father and brother; my youngest stepdaughter moved out of state to live with her mom full time at the age of twelve; five days before our wedding, a car accident left my oldest stepdaughter in a coma; and our own daughter needed two brain surgeries at the age of four to treat a rare and benign tumor. It was shortly after this event that I had enough.

The impact of these various life events, each with their own set of emotional baggage and family dynamics to consider, took a toll on our new marriage and family. We had no time to work on our marriage or blended family amidst all the chaos. Coupled with the insecurities we each brought into the marriage, we were not always the most supportive or compassionate to each other in our grief or sadness. And for me, through all of this, I still needed to figure out my role as a stepmom. In between all those events, life itself was still happening. As a result, it was a complicated and emotional decade full of worry, defensive positioning, and misunderstandings.

By 2009, my thoughts swirled uncontrollably with regret, irrational fears, resentment, and self-loathing. I was in a constant battle with my thoughts, which left me feeling extremely stuck, angry at the path I was on, and lost. I was conditioned to "stuff" uncomfortable and heart-wrenching experiences, feeling it was a weakness to vulnerably share my faults and fears. I was constantly frustrated with myself that I could not get back to the "normal me," which just perpetuated the cycle. Once we were past our daughter's medical issues, and life was back to normal, I realized the impact plowing through those feelings the prior decade had on my mental state. I was no longer able to function within what I perceived as the "drama of the blended family."

What We Think About is Who We Become

If only I had known about life coaching and the power of connecting with other stepmoms so I could have sorted through all the "drama" to determine what was real versus perceived, and what was in my control versus not.

What I know now is that our thoughts, feelings, and actions are all connected. Sometimes, our thoughts drive our feelings, while other times our feelings drive our thoughts — any which way, each one impacts the other. It is a cycle. Each day would confuse me more: how should I act, what am I allowed to do or say, what can I control, what about my feelings, why won't he let me "in," when can I say what I think, why do they ask for my help one day and ignore me the next, why can't I stick up for myself, what did I do wrong now, and when do I begin receiving?

Because I was focused so much on what was not going right, I was consumed with negative thoughts which generated feelings of sadness, isolation, frustration, and guilt. Feeling this way would make me act in ways I was not proud of, nor that felt like the "real me." I was resentful, defensive because I felt *they* had to change, and acting like a victim. In all reality, the swirl of these negative thoughts kept me from seeing another's perspective or understanding my role in the mess. My perception of all the drama was my only reality, and I was ready to leave.

Yet as I was looking around during Christmas 2008, I realized that despite the unrepairable mess I was perceiving, there was a strong foundation of love and connection I could not imagine living without. Throughout the years, my husband demonstrated his commitment to keeping our girls close and he was an amazing father. I really loved each one of them, and I did want us to stay together. Despite all the craziness, we still had a strong family. I was committed to my husband, stepdaughters, and keeping my family together. I just needed to get out of the negative swirl.

Time to Wake Up

As Charles R. Swindoll, a pastor and educator, believed, "Life is ten percent about what happens, and ninety percent how you react to it." It was in a Weight Watchers meeting a few months later in 2009 that my leader shared she was becoming a life coach. I had never heard of life coaching and quickly realized how much I craved the personal attention and clarity that would result from working with a life coach. She helped me realize that as life is happening, we have a daily choice in how we react to it. We just need help sorting through and navigating it, and that is the role of a life coach.

My journey towards owning my role in my unhappiness began that June when I made the choice to engage in my own personal development journey by attending a "Life Potentials" weekend at iPEC, my eventual coach training school. The more I learned about life coaching, the more I was drawn to it as a potential career. This opportunity was two-fold for me. I realized that by developing my own self-awareness I was acknowledging the only person's actions or attitude I could control was my own. And I really felt that one day, as I had a love for teaching, I would want to help others do the same.

I finally woke up and owned just how much I pretended in my life—to keep the peace, to make others like me, and to fit in. I realized how much unnecessary guilt I had for things that were out of my control. I learned that for me to find my right path, I had to first focus on getting to know *me*. This was going to require self-love and self-care. Not self-care as in a massage or reading a good book, but *real* self-care—defining who I was and what I wanted, defining my boundaries, finding reasons to love myself, and embracing my uniqueness. I needed first to understand and love myself before I could start expecting to feel love and understanding from others.

Making the Choice to Control My Future

I used to feel guilt for the way my journey played out. I now realize that no matter how it played out, if I hadn't had the journey I did and didn't love my family so much that I wanted so deeply to make things better, I would have never sought help through life coaching or the program. My journey and role as a stepmom oddly enough provided me an opportunity to get to know *myself* better. All we can control is our future, so we need to be grateful for the past that got us here!

Understanding where my unhappiness was coming from, accepting my role, acknowledging and offering compassion to others in the family for their journey, and reframing to a more positive mindset were key to my move forward. In all things, there is a purpose. I chose to let go of any regret and focus instead on creating a new dynamic by recounting all the experiences, decisions, and things I did that had a positive impact on my stepdaughters and others in my blended family. I had made a difference, and as a family, we make a difference.

Accepting Myself and My Journey Opened the Door

Thanks to my personal development, life coaches, and new support system, within a couple years I was taking risks to move me towards a future that included a focus on family, a career as a learning and development consultant and life coach, continued personal development, and a mission to positively impact the lives of many without compromising my authentic self. I am now living that crazy meaningful life while having stronger and authentic relationships within my blended family.

I let go of trying to control what was going to be and began to appreciate the mystery and power that comes from not always knowing what comes next but knowing no matter what does, I will handle it. I let go of trying to solve anyone else's relationships within my blended family. They all came with their own set of life experiences, beliefs about my role and theirs, assumptions about me and each other, and their own relationship with themselves. I could only accept that their perception did not have to be my reality, nor mine theirs. I can only control my own self-awareness, intentions, and attitude, and hope that by doing so, I exude the positive, reinforcing energy needed to keep healthier relationships within my family.

I love my stepdaughters immensely, and am grateful for their patience and support as we worked as a team to get where we are today—one unique, cohesive, and loving family. A sign has hung on my kitchen wall for sixteen years and I now see it was a mantra for our journey: "We might not have it all together, but together we have it all."

I am so passionate to help others who are considering the important role of a stepmom, and those stepmoms who resonate with how I was feeling while deep in my journey. Imagine what would be different if as parents and prospective stepparents we sat down together to discuss our roles, expectations, raw feelings, assumptions, underlying beliefs, insecurities, and vision for the future of our family and wellbeing of the kids? It is my personal mission to provide guidance and support to help stepmoms through their own personal development journey while navigating their new, complex role.

Sharon M. Wilson

Learning & Development Consultant / Personal-Professional Development Coach / Altruist

Any given week, you will find Sharon consulting with her corporate clients on a variety of learning and development topics, collaborating with colleagues to create and facilitate life-altering learning experiences, assisting clients in packaging their experience, coaching clients on career transition or relationships, volunteering at her daughter's school or driving her to soccer practice, designing inspirational gifts for her and her daughter's craft business, or creating memories with family and friends.

Sharon has broken through significant limiting beliefs to continue to create the "crazy" meaningful life she imagined, and wants to help others realize their potential, and right, to do the same! Sharon has contributed twenty-five years to the corporate, healthcare, education, and not-for-profit sectors in a variety of roles and leadership positions. She was always inspired by and drawn to professional opportunities to teach and mentor. Her life-changing experience as a stepmom provoked her belief that she could transform these interests into a career as she became a certified Professional Coach and Energy Leadership Master Practitioner through iPEC, started her own company ALIGN Training and Coaching, and pursued a MS degree in management and organizational behavior.

Sharon's most recent endeavors include: Inspire the Soul, an inspirational gift business she has started with her teen daughter. Creating Harmony in the Blended Family, a coaching program designed specifically to assist stepmoms in navigating the relationships within their blended families. Breaking My Boundaries, an empowering woman's conference designed to help women conquer their limiting beliefs.

Sharon M. Wilson
ALIGN Training & Coaching
P.O. Box 662
Grayslake, IL 60030
847-714-6245
sharon@aligntc.com
www.aligntc.com

Maryellen Klang

The Comeback Is Always Stronger
Than the Setback

It was the time my life! I had a wonderful and loving husband, a beautiful new home with his three amazing sons, three adorable little Shih-Tzu dogs, a fantastic job, great friends, and very healthy finances. It was a life I cherished living in Minneapolis, MN. I was in my mid-thirties, secure, happy, and loved.

Little did I know that it was all just too good to be true.

My family and I had barely recovered from my father's death in March 1990 when my husband suddenly left me for another woman in September of the same year. We had been trying to have a baby. I wanted to be like every other woman I knew, a mother. We were not successful.

I loved and trusted him more than words could define and his betrayal crushed my heart. He was a man who told me he loved me every single day. So his infidelity was the most devastating loss I ever experienced.

I hit rock bottom, crying every morning as I drove to work and every night when I drove home. I put on a good facade every day at work because I was the boss and didn't want people gossiping about me. I continued to shed tears when I got home each night. I knew deep in my soul that I could never believe in him or trust him again.

My family and friends were outraged as they witnessed his abandonment of me. My mother was exceptionally angry at him because she loved him too. It hurt her deeply to see my sadness and heartache that he caused me.

Christmas that year was extremely hard. I spent the holidays with my mother and siblings. I was lost and didn't know what to do. I leaned on my mother for advice and told her I wasn't sure what my next steps would be. She calmly said, "If you don't know what to do, do nothing. Just wait. The answer will come to you."

My mom, knowing I was depressed, encouraged me to go to Washington, DC with friends for the New Year. Before I left, she told me she wanted to give me two things. One was a photo of me in kindergarten when I was five years old. She told me my father carried that picture in his wallet for thirty two years. The other item was a small 1991 American Express Company pocket calendar.

I was puzzled as to why those items were so important for her to give to me that day. She knew I missed my father and she had retired from American Express where we both had worked, she for over 20 years. As we hugged and kissed each other goodbye, she looked straight into my eyes and told me she loved me. I told her I loved her too.

I had no way of knowing those words would be the last ones we would ever speak to each other.

I received a chilling call the next evening from my sister. She was crying, having to break the news to me that our mother had suddenly died. I was completely devastated and in shock.

My mother, my best friend, was now gone forever. Her passing threw me into the total depths of sadness and despair. She left me at the time when I needed her more than ever. For the first time, I found myself abandoned, scared and alone. I couldn't fathom why my life changed so quickly and what I had done to deserve it.

The only thing that was clear to me was that the idyllic life I led was now over. My husband's betrayal and my parents' deaths left me at a fork in the road with emotional wounds that ran deep.

The advice my mother had given me the last day I saw her alive proved to be true just one month after. I received a phone call from a headhunter asking if I was interested in interviewing for a job in Chicago. Asking if I was able to relocate, I slowly said yes. I was intrigued by who had referred me but he couldn't share who that was as it was confidential.

I decided to pursue the opportunity and flew to Chicago for the interview. I liked what I heard, however, starting over at age thirty-seven in a new city where I had no family or friends was never on my radar. After I interviewed, I emotionally broke down at the Water Tower in Chicago, locking myself in a bathroom stall where I cried for hours. I was just too overwhelmed, sad and depressed with the changes my life had taken in such a short time.

After weighing the pros and cons with myself and my family, I accepted the job offer and acted on faith rather than fear that this would be the right move for me. In retrospect, my shift to Chicago was actually the best and most positive step I had taken in months. I found Chicago to be a vibrant and diverse city that reminded me of NYC, smaller and more manageable. I felt alive again.

I found a beautiful apartment on the north side of the city overlooking Lake Michigan in a building called The New York. It was the only one in Chicago that would allow my three dogs.

Living there brought me back to life.

I started to meet all kinds of people who were diverse, interesting and friendly. When I walked my dogs, I was surrounded by others doing the same. Wrigley Field was just three blocks away and many Chicago Cub players also lived in the building. The building had a buzz that was just what I needed.

I started my new job and slowly started to make new friends. I went out by myself for the first time to parties or events. My family and friends visited and everyone agreed I was on the road to recovery.

I still had many lonely and sad days and nights that I got through one at a time. I walked for miles along the lake front, which was comforting. It was also a private place for me to mourn.

A turning point in my life occurred when I connected with my sibling's sister-in-law Carol who had moved to Chicago a few years prior. She lived in the suburbs and was a very independent woman, living a life of fun and adventure. She took me under her wing and invited me to go to dance clubs, which was a novelty for me.

I shared I really didn't know how to "go out" and that I had nothing to wear to a club. So we went shopping for new, sexy clothes that made me feel attractive and better suited my new single life.

The truth is that Carol saved my life. She infused fun and energy into my sad persona and gave me the push I needed to move forward. I was appreciative to be out and in her presence where we had fun and met all kinds of interesting people.

One night, I met Michael, an attractive man who invited me for a drink. We hit it off and started to date, which was a much needed boost to my ego. We ended up being together for over two years, enjoying all that Chicago offered and traveling to Europe on some wonderful trips. However, my heart was still seeking marriage and children, and his was not. So we parted ways.

It was in 1994 that I was offered a new job at American Express in Chicago. I took that opportunity, moved to the suburbs and began again. I loved my new job but was still fixated on finding Mr. Right and getting remarried. I was tired of being alone and surrounded by an office filled with women having babies and raising children.

As years passed, I finally accepted the fact that having a baby was not in the cards for me. And as I got older, it was no longer a possibility.

I eventually met my husband, Jim, in 2002. I had joined Match.com a year prior and he reached out to me in September. He seemed okay, except he wasn't living in Chicago. He expected to move to Chicago soon, but I was not in the mood to start a long distant relationship. And to top it off, his profile didn't thrill me—he was a scientist and I felt I had nothing in common with him.

It was on the twelfth anniversary of my father's death, March 18th, when Jim contacted me again at work after a long day. I was in my office, surrounded by my team, when his call came in. Upon hearing that the call was personal, they quickly dispersed and ran out of my office. He asked me out and I agreed to meet him, but only for a cup of coffee.

The night we met he persuaded me to at least have a drink and I relented. We went to a lovely restaurant in Oakbrook called Mon Ami Gabi. He met me with a white rose in his hand and persuaded me to at least let him get a table for us rather than sit at the bar.

As fate would have it, we ended up speaking for three hours. At the end of the evening, I hugged him and said I had a good time. He contacted me the next morning through Match.com, asking for my home number. I gave it to him and the rest is history.

We got engaged on the one year anniversary of our first date. My family and friends were thrilled that I had finally met a wonderful man who loved me and that we were getting married. He was the first man I had dated who totally treated me with respect and dignity. He was also the only man who did everything right.

We had a beautiful wedding ceremony at Grant Park in Chicago at the Rose Garden, surrounded by our family and friends.

We have been married now for fourteen years. I am grateful for him and his love that I know is real and will never fade, along with his integrity, intelligence and zest for life.

It has taken me years to write this story. I think back to the decisions, mistakes and crossroads that led me to where I am today. It was painstaking for me to learn how to live alone, support myself and make my own life full, but I did it and came out stronger in the end.

I have detached myself from the emotional pain of my past. I choose to surround myself with people who are positive and those who cherish family and friendships. I am fortunate to feel secure with my husband's love, knowing he will never hurt me. We live a very fulfilling and happy life together.

It's still natural for me to speculate about the person who recommended me for the job in Chicago years prior. I will never know who it was. What I do know is that person gave me the gift of starting over, which allowed me to emerge smarter and stronger from the saddest time of my life.

I will always treasure the gifts my mother gave me the last Christmas we spent together, my kindergarten picture and the 1991 American Express Company pocket calendar. She knew then, deep in her heart and soul, she and my father would guide me through the tumultuous and joyous times of my life, and my path would lead back to American Express, where I was destined to work until I retired.

I also know her parting gifts to me were ones that reflected my past and my future, and ones only a loving mother would know to give her daughter the Christmas that she died.

Maryellen Klang

Maryellen grew up in Brooklyn, NY and lived in that area for the first thirty years of her life. She graduated from Brooklyn College cum laude with a Bachelor of Arts Degree in Education. She also holds a Masters of Business Administration from Loyola University Chicago.

Working in the corporate business travel field led her to Chicago and being a director and People Leader for American Express Business Travel. Her achievements were mentoring and developing employees, leading diversity programs, and realizing excellent results for customer and employee retention. She was recognized for her efforts by earning multiple Presidents' Club Awards, along with Centurion Club and Diversity honors.

Maryellen strongly believes in giving back to the community in which she lives and works. She spearheaded American Express' Corporate Travel

Giving Campaign for five years. She now volunteers by serving on the board of directors for a non-profit agency based out of Wheaton, IL whose primary mission is to provide and mobilize services needed to strengthen families and communities in Chicago and Du Page County.

Maryellen now resides in Winfield, IL with her husband, Jim, and their pet dog, Lillie, a beautiful red and white Irish Setter. They enjoy spending time with their family, grandchildren and friends, while also take advantage of all that the diverse city of Chicago offers, along with traveling throughout the world.

Maryellen Klang
28W181 Belleau Drive
Winfield, IL 60190
331-223-1016
meklang@comcast.net

Stephanie Kurokawa

Finding Meaning Through Your Mess...

For as long as I remember, my life was about rules, accomplishments, and not bringing shame on my family. As a fourth generation Japanese-American female, that was a tall order to live up to. Accomplishments meant excellent grades and excelling at everything academic.

That's where I lowered the bar. In seventh grade, I was told I had a reading comprehension problem. Translation...I wasn't smart. Where my friends were at the top of the grade point average with honors classes and straight As, I struggled with keeping my grades average.

Feeling like I couldn't keep up, I immersed myself in sports and being creative. It gave me an outlet to escape and feel like I was good at something. All the things that don't make Asian parents proud. I even remember a time where my father asked, "Who are you?" To which I said, "AMERICAN." That led to a huge lecture.

The only thing that did was create a huge identity crisis which led me to feel isolated, disconnected, and wanting to be someone else. There were times I wanted to walk around with a bag over my head so people couldn't see me based on physical appearance.

I needed to be proud of being Japanese, but I didn't look it. The tape that continuously played in my head was, *I was not enough*.

Not...

smart enough

thin enough

pretty enough

white enough

Asian enough (whatever that means)

and, the best one of all...

not short enough. Most of my friends were shorter than me.

My thoughts created internal conflicts that led to low self-esteem, no confidence, and self-loathing. I felt disconnected. There was always a sense of separation between my day to day life and the one I lived at home.

I survived by creating two distinct personalities. East was who I needed to be whenever I was at home or within the community. West was who I was within my day to day encounters. West was free and creative, where East was restricted and confined.

Just to clarify, I don't have a personality disorder. I had to figure out a way to keep everyone around me happy. The separation created a huge divide with my identity issues.

Without the grades, I would always struggle academically. I knew I could never follow a traditional route. Entrepreneurship would be the way to accomplish my dreams.

After school, I landed a job in an advertising agency where I met a man who would serve as a mentor. He offered me a job, so I left the agency, and after a couple of years, I went out on my own. Finally, my dream to be an entrepreneur. It turned out to be the best decision I made.

I had an incredible life. On paper, I had everything I set out to accomplish. A successful career and business, my own home, great car, and money in the bank. I achieved and accomplished everything I could have ever imagined. Mission accomplished.

However, I wasn't fulfilled. There was something missing in my life and

I decided to find it. My friends were married with kids. I took the plunge, got married, and had kids. This had to be the missing piece. During this time, I walked away from my career…because isn't that what we women are supposed to do? Family over career?

Once I left the business, I started to implode. My career and business were a huge part of my identity. Being creative and competitive were the driving forces in my life. I believed it was an all or nothing game—as a woman, I believed you couldn't have both and be successful.

With that gone I had no escape and fell into the mom stereotype of what "rules" I needed to live by. I was on a new court, playing by everyone else's rules, and it was a game I couldn't win.

My identity was rooted in my career and being successful, now a huge void needed to be filled. During this transition, my thoughts quickly reverted to *not enough*. This time, it was deeper because I never dealt with the issues in the first place. With the *not enough* of growing up, a new list was added.

Now it was…

not thin enough

not contributing enough financially

not providing enough

not being a good enough mother

I had no vision, no goals, and no self-worth. I started a downward spiral, isolating myself from my closest friends. Instead of seeking comfort, I suppressed everything. Whatever I felt, I bottled it up, placed it on a shelf, and neatly packed everything away. I pretended that life was great, until life came crashing down and I had no idea who I was.

Looking in the mirror, I had no idea who was staring back. It was like pieces of a puzzle left to be picked up, only a shadow of someone I vaguely remembered remained. I created a false perception of who I needed to be. That perception created a reality that I lived just to gain the approval of my family and others.

I've found that perception only creates an illusion, and when that illusion is shattered, what we see is not the perception we created. What we see is the end result. It could be a life lived in quiet desperation or a life lived in struggle and the transformation. Of course, the latter is what we hope for.

In January 2011, I was served divorce papers. It wasn't a shock…I already knew divorce proceedings had started. During this time, a mix of emotions, both good and bad, washed over me. Finally, a chance to move on with my life—after all, I hadn't been happy for years.

I was a stay at home mom without a full-time income and had been out of the advertising industry for at least ten years.

How would I survive?

Interesting word "survive." I had been doing that for the past twenty years. Just surviving. I couldn't say it was much more than that. Between the kids and life, my thought was *just get me through the day.*

Don't get me wrong, there were moments of joy—the birth of my daughters, holidays, and those momentous firsts parents live for. With kids, careers, and life, there really wasn't much more.

Life was about survival and a lot of unconscious living. Served with those papers, survival turned to overwhelming panic and questioning how I would move forward through this process. By this time, our home had turned into a war zone. Everyone was picking sides to see who would end up faring better than the other. On a good day, our relationship was contentious at best, tearing our family apart.

Based on what I was seeing and the games being played, I knew it wasn't going to be pretty. There was no equity in our marriage. We didn't have things in common, we had different value systems, and the relationship was not built on a solid foundation.

After a few more visits with lawyers, I had a clear picture of what was in front of me. I hit the divorce trifecta, and it wasn't financially rewarding. Not only would I be dealing with divorce, I would also have to file for bankruptcy and go through foreclosure.

That wasn't the worse part—knowing my youngest daughter would have to go through the divorce trifecta was devastating. Once I knew my fate, I asked if she wanted to live with her father because I knew it could get really horrible. I felt like the cards were stacked against me. At that point, I didn't know if I would be living on the streets or in my car.

I remember the day my divorce was finalized. Sitting in my car, an emotional wave of relief washed over me as tears began streaming down my face. I was finally able to exhale, knowing that my fate was once again in my hands.

Looking at those papers, I knew the answers were staring me in the face. It had nothing to do with losing everything, it was that I didn't play full out. I was sitting in the stands, not fully engaged in my life. I told myself I wasn't enough so I settled for less than I deserved.

I played small because I gave up on my dreams and vision of who I could become. I allowed what other people said to run my life. As I searched for answers, I realized it wasn't what other people said to me that mattered, it was what I said to myself.

I didn't take responsibility for my choices and blamed others for where I stood. At that point, I decided to draw a line in the sand, take responsibility, make conscious choices, and learn to say no.

Starting over gave me a new perspective on life. Losing it all doesn't mean you've failed. Life has a way of teaching us that we aren't living up to our fullest potential. It gave me permission to not be perfect and the opportunity to grow into a better person.

Through the process, I immersed myself in self-development, worked on my spirituality, and got my head back in the game. It was while working on my self-discovery that I heard Tony Robbins' *Unleash the Power Within* was coming to town and I knew I had to go.

It wasn't about the fire walk. Though walking on 2000 degrees of burning coals does tend to make you think twice. It's a metaphor for the fears that stand in your way. I realized that the only way to move forward through the divorce was to face that fear.

During the fire walk, I learned that what we focus on and what we say to ourselves impacts what we can accomplish. Learning to change our internal dialogue is critical to success. When we focus on the fire (or the fear) we are paralyzed. Learning to focus beyond that (the end result) gives us the ability to see those possibilities.

One of the greatest lessons learned is that our experiences are either a lesson or a gift, and sometimes the lesson is our greatest gift. We choose how we move forward through life challenges.

Divorce allowed me to see that I wasn't fully engaged in my life. Still following the "rules" and looking for approval from others created a huge barrier to fulfilling my needs. Who we are isn't about the rules, accomplishments, or whether we make others proud. It's about living the life we design, fulfilling our deepest desires, and finding a deeper purpose to why we are here.

The lesson of divorce was the greatest gift anyone could have ever given me. It allowed me to see the magic of who I am. Those challenges have created a stronger sense of who I am, the boundaries I have put in place to protect myself, and most importantly...the power to control what comes into my life.

I believe my life has come full circle. The ability to control negative beliefs and replace them with more empowered, intentional thoughts has created an inner peace. Learning about re-wiring the brain, or neuro-retraining, has allowed me to play a bigger game, closing the gap that once existed. Until I was willing to change, my life would always stay the same.

Every day is a continuous learning experience where nothing is either right or wrong. I don't live in the space of perfectionism, which once kept me rooted in never feeling good enough. I get to choose every minute of every day, to grow and be the best version of myself.

This quote sums it all up:

"Your time is limited, so don't waste it living someone else's life. Don't be trapped by dogma - which is living with the results of other people's thinking. Don't let the noise of other's opinions drown out your own inner voice. And most important, have the courage to follow your heart and intuition. They somehow already know what you truly want to become. Everything else is secondary." — Steve Jobs

Stephanie Kurokawa

At an early age, Stephanie Kurokawa knew she was destined to become an entrepreneur. Fulfilling this dream, she worked with advertising agencies and studios in Chicago, Illinois and Los Angeles, California. During those years, she worked on brands like Apple, Honda, Budweiser, Marlboro and Playboy, which created her fascination with branding.

The love of brands ignited her passion to study the works of Tony Robbins, Jack Canfield and John Assaraf during a time of personal transition. She became involved in Toastmasters, where she earned her DTM (Distinguished Toastmaster) designation after a few short years and is a co-founder of Midwest Speaking Professionals.

She studied Strategic Intervention coaching through Tony Robbins of Robbins Madanes coaching, neuro-plasticity (retraining your brain) with John

Assaraf and is a certified Jack Canfield Success Principles Trainer. Combining strategic coaching with success principles, she creates strategies to systemize success for personal transformations.

She enjoys working out, biking, zip-lining, going to seminars, reading, quiet time by the lake and the moments she spends with her daughter.

Connect with Stephanie here:
LinkedIn: www.linkedin.com/in/stephaniekurokawa
Twitter: www.twitter.com/StephKurokawa
Facebook: www.facebook.com/snkurokawa

Stephanie Kurokawa
101 Lindenwood Court
Vernon Hills, IL 60061
847-721-6787
stephanie@StephanieKurokawa.com
www.StephanieKurokawa.com

Luanne Triolo Newman

Making a Difference & Inspiring
Others to Do the Same

What if a stranger asked you for help? Would you even consider it, or would you merely dismiss it? And how would it make you feel? A stranger named Pat once asked me for help, and little did I know what impact it would have on me.

It was 1992 and I was on my meal delivery route as a volunteer for DuPage Senior Citizen's Council, sometimes known as Meals on Wheels. I don't like to think of Pat as a stranger, but at first, of course he was. Pat was jolly, had a bright face and, similar to my ancestors, he emigrated from Italy. Argentina instead of America was where he first landed, and I always found that intriguing.

One day, after delivering his hot meal and cold milk, Pat told me he didn't have enough food to eat, even with the meal delivery, and asked me to help him. When I returned home, the weight of his request sunk in. I made some inquiries and found two food pantries that would allow him to visit each month. I decided I would take him there; I would help Pat.

Growing up, my mother would help others with her talents or her food. My older sister recently reminded me that Mom had repeatedly taken food to three of our cousins who had lost their mother at the young age of twenty-eight. I had witnessed that and other outreach she modeled for me at church and in the community. You could say she planted a seed with her actions.

I had never visited a food pantry as a guest, although as a troop leader our Girl Scouts packed food at the Bethlehem Center, later to be called the Northern Illinois Food Bank. When Pat and I made the two monthly stops, pantry personnel allowed him two grocery bags loaded past the top most months, but some months only one bag was offered.

My family and I had owned our newly-built home for five years at this point. Our neighbors all moved into their houses within a year of each other. They were kind and friendly people, open to meeting each other here or there and greeting all. My thoughts went back to the limited food at the pantry and I thought my neighbors might be able to afford to donate food, and I thought there was a chance they would.

The Brookstone Food Drive came out of this idea but had to be created from the ground up. Details had to be discovered—**when** to hold it, **what** food or items to collect, **where** the food was to go. In actuality, it really was not that difficult. It all fell into place.

We determined mid-May was the perfect time—late enough in the Spring to be past the cold but before families went away for summer. Without consulting anyone I made a list of non-perishable food items, paper goods, cleaning products, and personal items.

An informational flyer was created and the paper had to be *bright,* so Astrobrights was my choice. A half-sheet, two-sided flyer would be stapled to Jewel plastic grocery bags. Once we chose the date and the bags with flyers were assembled, the challenging task of tying them on each of the three hundred front doorknobs was next. Some years, my children or neighborhood kids helped. Some years, I covered three hundred homes after work or on weekends—it seemed to take forever, but the very best part was ahead.

The signs went up a few days ahead of the drive date. A *bright* poster board sign was at each and every exit of our neighborhood that read *BROOKSTONE FOOD DRIVE – This weekend at your mailbox.* This, I hoped, would be a last-minute reminder to neighbors when going to the store or gathering the items in their bags.

That Saturday seemed like it would never arrive! The flyers on the bags instructed generous neighbors to put the bags out at the foot of their mailboxes between 10 a.m. and 2 p.m. We didn't plan on going out earlier than that, but when we glanced down the street, those bright flyers were waving at us, inviting us to drive by and pick them up. We hopped in the car, the back hatch of the Toyota mini-van up as we slowly went down each street, squealing with delight to see bags out at the street. They had done it! We asked for help and they said yes with their bags. That is a feeling I will never forget and it is the most rewarding part of this effort.

After numerous trips to drop off the collected bags into the garage, we wanted to measure the success. We had a bathroom scale on the garage floor with a sliding pile of food-filled plastic bags. My daughter was on the scale, being handed five or six bags at a time. "Ten pounds," I called out while my son quickly wrote the number on a pad of paper. "Eight pounds," and so on until all bags were weighed. A quick tabulation of the column of figures delivered the success in a number. Three hundred pounds was the sum!

Then we were off to the food pantry, where they were expecting us even though it was a late Saturday afternoon. Two cars were loaded then quickly unloaded with the help of three kids. Upon return, time was taken to staple an addendum to those *bright* neighborhood signs: *300 POUNDS COLLECTED – BRAVO, BROOKSTONE!*

Happy but exhausted, the letter to the editor of the local paper would have to wait a day. Nonetheless, it was carefully crafted to thank those who volunteered and donated, but also challenged and offered assistance to another neighborhood who might consider taking on a similar project.

The years passed. Numbers of collected items grew. Children grew, too. Different friends and their kids cycled in to help, and with them they brought a new excitement. As word spread, the number of pounds also increased: 350, 412, 740, 842, and in its eleventh year, the Brookstone Food Drive produced

881 pounds of donated food, paper, and personal products.

A divorce would necessitate the sale of the house and the end of me at the helm of the food drive. With some convincing, some neighbor boys kept the tradition going for an additional five years, finishing in 2008. It made me feel extremely good that it kept going, and, maybe, it took away a bit of guilt I felt by leaving it behind.

Life went on. I was in the workforce and part of the Rotary Club of Carol Stream (IL) for seven years when it was my "turn" to slide into the president position in the club. Rotary is an international service organization founded in 1905 in Chicago by Paul Harris, whose motto is "Service Above Self," and now attracts 1.2 million members in 220 countries across the world.

It was explained to me that it's customary for the president to bring a project of their own to the club and I was asked if I had anything in mind. It was always clear to me that my Brookstone food drive project could be expanded to other neighborhoods, to include businesses, schools, and more. "Do you think it would work?" fellow Rotarian Bob asked me.

October 10, 2009 was the first Community-wide Food Drive sponsored by the Rotary Club of Carol Stream. Spreading the word was fun and easy and included community meetings held at the Village Hall where residents could hear how they might fit in to this event. Each subsequent year, the process was more streamlined. Additional resources were added, including volunteers manning a table outside of multiple grocery stores in town, and explaining the event taking place that very day all across our village.

Feeding America 2015 data shows that 7.3% of the population in DuPage County, Illinois is "food insecure" and in need of help. That rate is below the state rate of 11.7% and the U.S. rate of 13.7%.

Businesses and schools that had been collecting for a month converged on the bus drive-up area of Glenbard North High School. Students, athletes, club members and even the mayor greeted them. Traffic flow was carefully considered to keep things moving as their vehicles were emptied of the many, many plastic bags with those **bright** flyers which were now yellow. Donors were handed a thank you card. Some had seen the huge electronic sign provided by the Village of Carol Stream. It had been sitting just near the bus drive-up area for a week, blinking the date and time of the Community-wide Food Drive, enticing those who passed to prepare: grab some food and bring it back on that one day when it was all to happen.

And happen it did! At 10:00 a.m. on the appointed Saturday, the first of the volunteers arrived. Tables were set up...and then more tables. And at 11:00 the first of the trucks from the schools would arrive. The food items were not sorted or counted; they were placed on tables to somewhat equal out three collections of food to be picked up by three local food pantries. In the later years, three township food pantries were added, since the collection grew.

The numbers of volunteers grew, too. It warms your heart to see a truck pull up and, immediately, willing hands are grasping the handles of grocery bags to load or unload, depending on the time of day. What would take you or me fifteen minutes and multiple trips back and forth to the truck can take only ninety seconds when ten teenagers attack it. Just another reminder that "many hands make light work," just as playwright John Heywood noted in the 1500s—it is still true in the twenty-first century.

April 22, 2017 was the eighth annual Community-wide Food Drive in Carol Stream. It was a sunny and warm day and all the tables were set up at the curb of the bus drive-up. Eighteen double lunchroom tables—three each for the six food pantries. Bags and boxes would be placed on top and when there was not another open spot, items were placed below each table, just so that there could be somewhat of an equal division of the food collected.

Eleven o'clock in the morning, those tables were empty and the first trucks pulled up. For four hours, students, athletes, moms and dads, scouts, Knights of Columbus, Club Interact, and members of the Rotary Club worked in unison to unload the items. Cooperation was at its very best. The spirit of community was evident! Then came the food pantries, scheduled to allow a staggered arrival to keep all from being overwhelmed. As tables were emptied, they were collapsed and returned to the building. One by one, they left.

Five o'clock and no tables were to be found and no food was left at the curb. More than **eighteen tons** of food was divided and picked up. All in, all out in six hours. What a community project; what a success!

Pat's needs inspired me to help him and others like him. It would never be possible for me to purchase or personally pick up eighteen tons of food. It took many hands. I didn't know that I had a passion to help those who are food insecure. It is incredible how many want to help others. When you call on them to join you in a mission, or a passion, it sparks something within them. You can feel it. You can see it: their *bright* and happy faces. They are part of something bigger…bigger than one person. Teamwork. Cooperation. Caring. Passion.

So, I ask you again, what if a stranger asked you for help? What about all those strangers who haven't asked you but who still are in need of your help?

What is **your** passion? How will you act upon it and make a difference? To paraphrase the late President Ronald Reagan, no one can "help everyone, but everyone can help someone." Who would you help, and who would *you* inspire?

Luanne Triolo Newman

Business Professional / Networking Aficionado / Marketing Executive / Event Planner / Community Leader

Born in Chicago and raised in the suburbs, Luanne was able to stay at home while raising three children. Involved in their school, scouts, and clubs, she honed her skills in volunteering and organization. A strong community volunteer in Carol Stream for over thirty-five years, Luanne lives and breathes community, where she has been the recipient of multiple awards and honors.

Helping business professionals forge relationships and being an advocate for local business, you can find Luanne working hard for the Carol Stream Chamber of Commerce. She loves her job!

Outside the chamber, she is a community leader active in many groups such as Rotary, 100+ Women Who Care, the Historical Society, Parade Committee, Citizen of the Year, and more. Amazed by the power of those who work together to help others, Luanne is hooked on helping.

Genealogy, travel, and lending a hand are all things Luanne is passionate about. "What is your passion and what effect can it have helping others?" is her question for you.

Luanne Triolo Newman
630-918-9008
luanne.newman@outlook.com

Freda McGhee

Back to the Basics

As a little girl growing up in South Florida, summertime brought memory-making opportunities for my sister, Nita, and me. We were used to sandy toes, balmy breezes, and barbeque ribs cooking on the grill. Hollywood was a growing suburb of Miami/Fort Lauderdale, so the "country life" was out of reach.

It was out of reach until our vacation began, that is. Our annual family vacation was always spent between two little podunk towns—compared to Hollywood—in North Carolina: Hildebran and Hickory. My roots and both sets of my grandparents grew deep into the soil in those places. I never realized, as a little girl, how precious those memories would become, and the life lessons that would follow.

Bubble Gum

Twelve hours in the back seat of a Toyota in the early 1970s with Nita and our dog, Spooky, could sometimes feel like an eternity. I recall the warm feeling that would wash over me as we exited the interstate and got on the road toward Shelby. The winding curves, the smell of sweet grass, and the lowing of cows—it was like coming home. But that's not what made me smile.

It was the bubble gum! My Papaw was a hard-working man. He and my Mamaw Hazel worked at a sock mill and they also ran a small farm. They were two of the most wonderful people I've ever known.

I don't think there was ever a time that we didn't drive down that long, winding, gravel driveway through the fields of hay to their little white house that Papaw built himself that there weren't two little brown bags sitting on Papaw's dresser. Nita and I would jump out of the car, give hugs and kisses to our grandparents, fling open the screen door, and fly like racehorses to their bedroom. I'm really not sure why there was always a race. But there was. I guess we both won, because we both always got a bag.

After grabbing our bags, we would open them up and there they were... big, round, colorful, juicy balls of bubble making goodness. Cherry, grape, watermelon, and sour apple—the kind with green spots. Such a small gesture, but such a big impact on two little girls!

Tree Climbing

Just outside the old kitchen windows, all that could be seen was the big old blue spruce. It towered higher than the house. In my little girl self, it seemed to tower to the heavens. It made the perfect hideout for Nita and me. I think we would even eat lunch out there sometimes. When I crawled through the low-hanging branches that rested on the ground like tired feet, I felt like those kids in Narnia must have felt. The branches began extending from the trunk, just inches from the ground. Since I have zero athletic talent, those low-growing branches were a gift. I was able to climb higher and taller than I could stand.

When Nita and I were tucked away in our blue spruce hideout, it was as if the rest of the world stopped. We dreamed and talked and laughed and ate lots of watermelon.

The Tractor

My Papaw had an old grey and red tractor. Sometimes, on really special days, I'd hear him holler, "Come on, Charlie. Let's go for a ride!" I'd drop whatever I was doing—playing jacks, making bead necklaces, or painting a paint-by-number picture—and head outside.

He would open up the big old creaky door to his hand-built garage. Dark, damp, and musty, I still recall the cool air that would be sucked out into the heat of a summer's day, hitting my face like a breath of not-so-fresh air. Carefully, I would go in, straight to the tractor. There was always a little bit of trepidation that entered with me, though. I never knew when a little white mouse might show its twitching pink nose.

Papaw would climb up on the old grey machine and then I would follow, right onto his lap. He would crank that baby up, and slowly maneuver us out into the sunlight, careful to not hit the sides of the doorway. Once outside, he would say, "Okay, Charlie, you steer." And off we'd go. My smile was as big as the rear tires on that old machine! My Papaw trusted me, and was always there to guide me along.

Trains

Down in South Florida, the nearest train tracks were miles away from where we lived. That was not the case while on vacation, though. Mamaw Starr lived in a house right by the train tracks. The only thing that separated her front stoop and the railroad ties was a dirt road.

Way back when I was around three or four years old, if I heard the rumbling of a train in the night or a blast of a train horn, I would dash out of bed, straight to Mamaw's room. Tapping her on the shoulder, I would wake her up. I didn't even have to say anything. She knew. Quickly, she'd put on her robe and slippers, put me on her hip, and carry me to the front glass door. We would watch the train until the caboose said goodbye. I would smile and give her a hug. And back to bed we would go.

It was a little different at the farm. The track sat down in the valley, down from where Mamaw Hazel and Papaw's house sat. It was too far to shake the house in the night, but during the day, I'd fly outside if I heard the train horn blow. I remember standing by the old well, looking out over the vegetable garden, and then past the cow pasture, all the way to the train tracks. And I would count. Nita and I would try to remember how many cars the longest train had each day. Things are so different in the country.

Osh Kosh B' Gosh

Families have traditions for their children as they pass through the years. Some birthdays hold a special significance. For some reason, my Papaw saw the number twelve as significant.

The summer I was twelve years old, he took me on a day trip deeper into the country. I was hoping for more bubblegum, but he had something much bigger in mind. He took me to a little old country store that was full of Osh Kosh B' Gosh overalls—in *my* size!

Papaw wore overalls six and a half days a week. A dress shirt and dress pants were much more fitting for church on a Sunday morning. When we walked into the store, he said, "Charlie, pick you out a pair of them overalls." That's the only gift, outside of bubblegum and birthday and Christmas gifts, he ever gave me. I don't know that it was ever a big deal to him, but it was to me. It sent me a message of value and importance. My Papaw liked having me around—for the most part!

Tickled Pink

With every childhood, there is a touch of rebellion. And when good parents are involved, there are always consequences. There is one particular night that stands out in my mind that Nita and I shared in some joint rebellion. Please know, we were always excellent law-abiding and rule following children. But sometimes...

We shared a bed in Mamaw Starr's guest bedroom. We were probably ten and fourteen years old, so definitely old enough to know better. We were laughing and talking after bedtime, and obviously had become too boisterous for our mom and dad. Daddy came in, with his stern voice—and slight grin—and told us that if we were going to stay in the same room, we would have to sleep with one of our heads at the head of the bed and one at the foot of the bed. It seemed logical to me.

Well, the sillies had already taken hold, so in our new position, after

Daddy left and closed the door, the tickling began. Our feet were so convenient for each other! Before we knew it, we were laughing loudly, legs flailing everywhere, and all of a sudden, we heard a loud thud and then my head was quickly sliding towards the floor. The slat had fallen out of the bed frame and the mattress tipped, so the foot of the bed was on the floor and the head of the bed was in the air. I'm sure it would have been quite a sight to behold. The belly laughs that followed were too large to contain. I'm not really sure what happened after that, but Nita and I have shared a number of laughs when recalling that night. Laughter is so important in this life.

So, What's the Purpose?

I've summed up my childhood memories and tied them to adulthood to make a beautiful tapestry of life. I hope you can connect the dots and benefit from some things I've learned along the way.

Bubble Gum—Through Papaw's kindness and consistency, I learned the importance of dependability and faithfulness. Papaw's consistency in providing bubble gum reminds me of God's faithfulness. Forever, O Lord, Your word is settled in heaven. Your faithfulness endures to all generations; You established the earth and it abides (Psalm 119:89–90).

Tree Climbing—Throughout my life, I've had many opportunities to find retreat for my soul, whether because of death, divorce, single-parenthood, unemployment, eating issues, indecisiveness about a career, or loneliness. God has used these blue spruce moments in my life to bring encouragement, healing, and restoration to my soul. Surely, I have calmed and quieted my soul, like a weaned child with his mother; like a weaned child is my soul within me (Psalm 131:2).

The Tractor—While a child, Papaw would give me guidance on the tractor. In my life since then, I have shifted my eyes to my Heavenly Father for guidance. Your ears shall hear a word behind you saying, "This is the way, walk in it," whenever you turn to the right hand or whenever you turn to the left (Isaiah 30:21).

Trains—As a child, I thought my life would turn out like Cinderella's. I thought the train tracks would be smooth and straight. I ended up struggling with weight issues for years. Divorce showed up at one of my train stations. Even a miscarriage jumped on the tracks. All unexpected by the little girl within, but it didn't surprise God at all. God is faithful, by whom you were called into the fellowship of His Son, Jesus Christ our Lord (I Corinthians 1:9).

Osh Kosh B' Gosh—Papaw cherished me. He went out of his way to let me know how much he loved me. Don't get me wrong, there were times I frustrated the stew out of him, but he always loved me. Just as I held a special place in Papaw's heart, I hold a special place in God's heart, too. For thus says the Lord of hosts: "He sent Me after glory to the nations which plunder you; for he who touches you, touches the apple of His eye" (Zechariah 2:8).

Tickled Pink—Silly as we were, Nita and I didn't engage in major rebellion the night we broke the slat in the bed frame. That came later in my life. Even though there have been times of rebellion in my adult life, I've realized that having a heart that is bent toward the obedience of God's truth is the most fulfilling way to live. The Lord is not slack concerning His promise, as some count slackness, but is longsuffering toward us, not willing that any should perish but that all should come to repentance (II Peter 3:9).

Freda McGhee

Life's twists and turns have provided Freda with many relatable experiences. As a mother of three girls, she is well-versed in the drama of the teen years, as well as the exhaustion of two in diapers simultaneously. Having one daughter living on her own, and one daughter married, she understands the effects of an emptying nest. Since her youngest daughter is now driving, the taxi driver hat has been retired.

As a daughter, she understands the responsibility and the joys of caring for her aging parents. She spends as much time as she can with them now that they live with her and her family.

As a wife, she has experienced highs and lows; fun times and challenges. She has survived divorce and has lived out faithful love and commitment.

As a teacher, she was a cheerleader for students with special needs. After fifteen years in the classroom, she has chosen to be at home to pursue writing and speaking opportunities.

As a speaker and author, she thoroughly enjoys sharing with her audience how she has made it through tough times in order to give encouragement and hope. Her walk with Jesus has proven to her that He is the only steadfast rock in this world.

As a graduate of the 2013 Christian Communicators Conference, she is prepared to share her experiences and the impact faith in Jesus Christ can have on a life.

Freda leads weekend retreats for ladies to encourage and bring hope to those who are struggling. Hands-on craft activities add an extra dimension to these special times. If you are interested in attending one of her retreats, please contact her through e-mail.

Freda McGhee
Freda McGhee - Life Trainer
Terrell Lane
Atlanta, GA 30549
770-560-9271
fullcirclefm@gmail.com
www.fredamcghee.com
Facebook - Freda McGhee - Life Trainer

Brenda Schmid

A Near Death Experience Saved My Life

On August 15, 2009, I was involved in a horrific boating accident. I was boating on The Chain of Lakes with friends when the boat I was on collided with another boat. The force of the crash caused my boat to capsize; I was trapped underneath it.

THE ACCIDENT

I remember it like it was yesterday. As I flailed under water, I wondered why I couldn't swim to the surface. I held my breath for as long as I could, then I couldn't hold it any longer. As I took my last breath and realized I was going to die, a wonderful sense of peace came over me. I told God that I was ready to go home, and I calmly gave up the ghost.

As it turned out, it wasn't my time to meet Jesus. There was a pontoon boat passing by at the time of the crash, and the owner of the boat dove into the water at least eight times before he felt my arm. He dragged me to shore, where two Marine Unit Officers were waiting. After five minutes of CPR, I finally started to breathe on my own. They estimated that I was under water for six to eight minutes.

I was then air lifted to a nearby hospital. I had sustained numerous injuries, including a broken nose, fractured sinus, a contusion on my C5 vertebrae, several facial cuts, and other neck fractures. The main concern, however, was the bruising of my spinal cord. This caused tingling and numbness throughout my entire body. My hands were sore, my fingers didn't work right, I couldn't walk, and my feet felt like they were wrapped in twine. As I started physical therapy, I kept hoping this was all a dream and that I would soon wake up.

THE POWER OF PRAYER

I prayed after my boating accident, but my prayers were probably not what you'd expect. Instead of thanking God for saving my life, I begged Him to end it. I was in a constant state of pity because of my broken body, and I had to wear a hard, ill-fitting neck brace that was incredibly uncomfortable. Also, I found out I had sustained a TBI (Traumatic Brain Injury) which affected my memory. With no husband or children to take care of me, I felt alone and afraid.

Since I refused to pray for my own healing, the Lord provided me with family and friends to do it for me. One week after my accident, my sister started a prayer chain at her school. Over one hundred people were constantly praying for me. Even now I think about this and am deeply humbled. My church friends prayed for me, too. Jean, Melanie, Kathy, Terri—they all prayed for my healing. Sometimes I would feel like I was literally covered in prayer. It was like lying under a warm, cozy blanket.

How do I know prayer works? Because in spite of myself, I kept experiencing miracle after miracle. During the period when I didn't want to live, I needed surgery on my fractured C5 vertebrae. I figured I wouldn't survive the surgery since my body was so damaged and broken, so I was looking forward to not waking up from the anesthesia. Not only did I wake up, but I woke up to hear that my neurosurgeon had to "go in sideways" since I had more inflammation than he'd anticipated. Against great odds, he had performed a successful fusion surgery.

After a few miserable weeks of living in my condo with caregivers, I went to live with my friend Cindy and her family in my hometown of Grand Rapids, Michigan. I started in-home occupational and physical therapy after a few more weeks. If I had wanted to die before, I wanted to die a thousand times more now. There I was, still in my hard neck brace, trying to walk while gripping Cindy's kitchen counter. I couldn't look down because of the neck brace, and I couldn't feel my feet because of all the nerve damage. I felt hopeless and, even worse, pathetic. It seemed to me that even the therapists thought I was a lost cause.

However, I worship a God of lost causes. Even as I kept begging the Lord to just take me home, my friends and family kept praying. One Saturday, a group of long-time friends came to visit me. They brought snacks and treats and tried to cheer me up. Broken and sad as I was, I laid down and went to sleep on the couch right in the middle of their visit. Just before they left, my friend Sherri woke me up and asked if she could pray for me. Naturally, I said yes. She prayed a beautiful prayer asking the Lord to help me walk again and heal my broken body. I remember feeling a deep sense of peace as she spoke these wonderful words. I knew right then and there that God was listening.

Once I graduated to just wearing the hard neck brace at night, my mood lifted considerably. Although I still had to use a walker, my legs felt stronger and my balance was starting to improve. For the first time in what seemed like forever, I felt hopeful.

THE POWER OF CARING, SUPPORTIVE FRIENDS

Since I am an extrovert and quite social, I've always had lots of friends; however, as I look back, I think I've always taken my friends for granted. I'd call them, they'd call me, we'd talk, we'd laugh, we'd go out, and so on and so forth. It's not that I didn't appreciate them, it's just that I didn't understand the true meaning of friendship. As soon as I had my accident, that all changed.

I've got two girlfriends who are super organized and good at taking charge. Sharon and Cindy were my angels. Lord knows I needed them, and they did not disappoint. As I lay there in my hospital bed, unable to move or make sense of anything, they started making phone calls and doing research. Since most hospitals want to release you as soon as possible, I needed to know how I was going to function once I got home since I couldn't walk or use my hands. I also needed somebody to help me wade through the whole insurance process, which is complicated even for the healthy. Lastly, I needed a good personal injury attorney, since it appeared that the accident was the fault of the other driver.

Sharon introduced me to her friend Kathleen, a nurse at the Chicago Institute of Neurosurgery. I needed a good, experienced neurosurgeon to repair my fractured C5 vertebrae, and she found me one of the best in the Chicagoland area. I needed an excellent personal injury attorney, and again, she found me an amazing lady. I truly don't know what I would have done without Kathleen. Besides finding me these excellent professionals, she was also such a good friend to me. She visited me in the hospital as often as she could, usually bringing with her a delicious treat. Since I had lost a lot of weight after the accident, she wanted to "fatten me up." She also introduced me to the fun of watching the Chicago Bears play football. One of my best memories during that time is watching the game with her one Sunday night.

When I lived with Cindy and her family, I was not a pleasant person to have around—I was cranky, demanding, and when I first arrived, smelly. All I really wanted to do was sleep; in fact, I slept so much that I developed bedsores. Cindy had to treat them, which I'm sure was not a pleasant task. I was terrified that I was going to have a bowel or bladder accident, so I insisted on wearing adult diapers. Even though she was exhausted herself, Cindy got me up every morning at six o'clock to take me to the bathroom. One morning, I had to urinate so badly that I decided to just go in my diaper, figuring the diaper would hold all the liquid. It didn't, so my bed ended up being a soggy, foul smelling mess. Cindy never complained, just changed my sheets and put me back to bed. She was truly a saint.

When I was well enough to go to outpatient physical therapy, I stayed with my sister and brother-in-law, Chris and Wes. Since they both worked, my nephew took me to therapy at Mary Free Bed, an excellent facility in Grand Rapids. This time spent with my family was so instrumental in my healing, both physically and emotionally. We had lots of fun watching TV, discussing politics and just laughing together. I grew stronger every day, and after a month of intensive physical therapy, I was finally able to throw out my walker. Brenda Schmid was back, and Brenda Schmid was going home!

THE POWER OF GRATITUDE

It has been nine years since my accident, and every morning I thank God for letting me live to see another day. I am just so grateful to still be here. Am I back to where I was before the accident? No, I'm not, but in some ways, I'm better. Nourison, my employer, held my job for me, so I went back to work as a sales representative in January of 2010. I have since retired, but I am so grateful that I was able to work again. Since I had a traumatic brain injury, my memory and concentration aren't what they were, but my mind is still sharp. I have Central Cord Syndrome, so I will be on strong medication for the rest of my life, but I am fully mobile and able to walk. My hands are stiff and sore, but I can do everything I did before the accident, it just takes longer. This is the new and improved Brenda Schmid, a woman who lives every day with a sense of gratitude.

Brenda Schmid

Brenda was born into a Christian family in Grand Rapids, MI, on Valentine's Day. From kindergarten until the day she graduated from Calvin College with a BA in sociology, she attended Christian schools. Brenda believes that her strong Christian foundation shaped her life in a positive, wonderful way.

Brenda moved to Chicago when she was in her late twenties. Quite by accident, she got into the flooring business and stayed there for the better part of twenty-five years. She was a marketing rep for Amoco Fabrics and Fibers and Wools of New Zealand, and a sales rep for Nourison Industries. All of these positions involved extensive travel, so she learned to organize her schedule, manage her time, manage a budget, and work by herself with little supervision.

In 1991, she married for the first and only time. They were happily married for many years, but his adultery ended the marriage in 2007.

For the last three years, she has been happily retired. Brenda has always loved animals, so she recently decided to become a guinea pig mommy. She currently has five of the adorable little rodents. Her goal is to write a series of children's books chronicling the lives of her piggies.

Since she no longer travels for work, she now has the time to volunteer at church and attend daytime Bible studies. She especially enjoys serving in the nursery on Wednesday mornings.

Her other two passions are classic rock concerts and leisure travel. Although she still has a long bucket list, she tries to take a major trip every year. Some of her most fun adventures have occurred in New Zealand, Egypt, Israel, Dubai, Bora Bora and Italy. Regarding classic rock, she usually attends between five and ten concerts every year.

Last but not least, Brenda is a huge Detroit sports fan and enjoys attending baseball and football games. Go Lions! Go Tigers!

Brenda Schmid
Palatine, IL 60074
224-532-3403
Brenda.schmid@icloud.com

WHERE ARE THEY NOW?

Getting Yourself Unstuck

When I learned about this project, I was already full into the writing, publishing, and marketing process of my other book, *Getting Yourself Unstuck;* however, I couldn't put everything in that book. *Overcoming Mediocrity* allowed me to publish a very personal story that was very difficult for me to accept in print and I didn't see fitting in my other book, yet I knew needed to be told.

As agonizing as it was for me to ink out my story, Christie and the DPWN Team stood beside me and made the publishing process so seamless and, dare I say, fun, because all I had to do was to follow their proven system. Now, as an Amazon best-selling author, both of my books work in tandem in my marketing process.

The comments I continue to receive since publishing my story is a powerful daily reminder that my story illuminates a real problem in our society and provides a proven solution. I continue to have people say to me, "Wow! I had no idea! I need to tell my sister-in-law, neighbor, niece..." People are reaching out to those with a child under the age of one or an older child who struggles with learning disabilities, autism, or other spectrum labels.

Plus, meeting and collaborating with a new group of resilient women turned out to be a very exciting honor.

My motto is, if you are not having fun, you are doing something wrong. Christie has a system that really works. All I had to do was to follow the bouncing smiley face (not literally of course).

Thank you, Christie and the DPWN Team.

Name: Angie Engstrom
Business Name: Life Design Brands LLC
Contact Email: Angie@AngieEngstrom.com
Website: www.AngieEngstrom.com
Volume: *Overcoming Mediocrity Resilient Women*

Side Dishes

I remember the conversations I had with Christie about participating in her upcoming *Overcoming Mediocrity* book. I really wanted to express my thoughts about healing personally as well as the transformational healing in my business so that my journey could inspire others. In addition, I felt that sharing my story in a book like this would provide me instant credibility and allow me to become someone people could relate to. I also wanted to leverage my new book to acquire speaking engagements where I could talk about real estate investing and education in order to grow my business. It sounded like this project would provide me with all of this, but I wanted to make sure my husband and business partner agreed with my decision.

Jay completely supported my decision and neither one of us has ever looked back. Since the publication of my book, I've received numerous notes from readers who were inspired by my story and thanked me for sharing. I also gained the confidence to contribute to another book with Jay. We wrote about our experiences as real estate investors. I am sure I would not have had the confidence to do that book had it not been for the guidance and support from Christie and her team.

Although I enjoy selling my books and giving them to close family members, I also found that I could trade them for books written by other author friends!

Overall, I gained a new level of credibility as a business woman from my peers and I keep uncovering additional ways that this book project has added value to my life!

Name: Nancy Abramovitz
Business Name: BTE Ventures
Contact Email: nancy.bte.biz@gmail.com
Website: www.BteVentures.biz
Volume: *Overcoming Mediocrity Resilient Women*

Failure Is Not an Option

My goals for participating in the Overcoming Mediocrity project were to expand my potential and my reach by meeting others like me. I was looking for a network of women who've been in my shoes at some point in their life and are willing to embrace, teach, guide, and support me on my journey. My biggest goal is to be able to offer that same light back to them in return.

I was surprised and pleased to hear that we made it into more categories than expected with our Amazon best-selling campaign, which has been a great tool in selling myself.

Name: Monique Hicks

Business Name: Vitality Med Spa and Plastic Surgery Center and Modrn Sanctuary

Title: CEO

Contact Email: MHicks@VitalityMedSpaMD.com, Monique@ModrnSanctuary.com

Website: www.VitalityMedSpaMD.com, www.ModrnSanctuary.com

Volume: *Overcoming Mediocrity Resilient Women*

Transformation

I joined the Overcoming Mediocrity team because I felt that if I could favorably impact one person's life by sharing my story, my job would be done. I was not sure what to expect, but I have to say that it was an overwhelmingly positive experience. Shortly after the book's release, I received multiple texts and emails thanking me for telling my story. One person in particular told me that she felt alone, depressed, and worthless during a recent bout of depression and my story made her realize that she was not alone.

I truly love being able to say I am an Amazon Best Selling Author because it has opened many doors for me. I'm excited to continue on my journey having just completed health coach training with the Institute for Integrative Nutrition. This book gave me the confidence to pursue a life-long passion and I will be forever grateful.

Name: Andrea M. Trovato

Contact Email: andrea@andreatrovato.com

Website: www.AndreaTrovato.com

Volume: *Overcoming Mediocrity Remarkable Women*

Informed Choices

Since the publication of my story "Informed Choices" in November 2016, my life has propelled to new heights. The story gave the world immediate access to my "why," which opened many doors for me. My goal has always been to provide the world access to a higher standard of healthcare — through chiropractic care. By the first quarter of 2017, in one week, I was simultaneously made an offer from an investor for my new business venture, Chiropractic Led Onsite Care, and a business development role by Medulla LLC, the healthcare management solutions for the world's leading chiropractic provider group, Chiro One Wellness Centers. I chose to align myself with Medulla LLC because they have the right people in the right seats driving the bus (inspired by Jim Collins).

Next, by September 2017, I was asked to be the co-program manager for the Young Entrepreneurs Academy (YEA!), a groundbreaking program that transforms local middle and high school students into real, confident entrepreneurs. By November 2017, I was nominated for the 2017 Keys to Success Hero/Heart Award for the Palatine Area Chamber of Commerce, and if that was not enough, in December 2017, accepted the nomination for chairperson for the American Diabetes Association 2018 EXPO. During this time, I was still coaching people on health and wellness, and helping them to lose weight and make informed choices about their wellbeing with dōTERRA Essential Oils.

My health journey is a compelling story, but none of this would have been possible without Christie Ruffino, who left no stone unturned; she optimized every opportunity for the authors to gain greater exposure and become Amazon Best Selling Authors. I am truly grateful for this once in a lifetime opportunity.

Name: Jodi L. Suson

Business Name: Medulla LLC & dōTERRA Essential oils

Contact Email: back2basics15@yahoo.com

Website: www.doterra.com/US/en/site/jodisuson

Volume: *Overcoming Mediocrity Remarkable Women*

Faith is the Backbone to our Blessings

I joined the OM Project in order to share my story of faith and the loss of my parents at two key times in my life. I wanted to encourage everyone who read my story that they are not alone, they are important, and that they have something to share that others need. I knew this would be a wonderful experience to help me publish other genres of writing such as poetry.

The goal was met through a simple process. I met Christie, and she helped with everything that was needed to be published in a very quick timeframe. I wrote about some times in my life that I cherish, that challenged and shaped me, and that influenced who I am in business, personally, and spiritually.

The benefits of my Amazon Best Selling Author status—I had an article published in the Sigma Kappa Triangle. It is a magazine that shares what is going on with the national sorority, it's philanthropies, alumni, and accomplishments of individuals. Sorority sisters near and far have contacted me to obtain the Overcoming Mediocrity Book with a personalized message inside from me. Another benefit from this status was to be able to meet, communicate, be motivated by and learn from other authors. Friendships and business relations have been and continuously are being developed. I am looking forward to writing another chapter for OM-Christian Women.

As a result of previous editing work on two Amazon projects for newer authors—one local novelist and one author of short stories and poetry in New Jersey—these experiences offered different creative ideas for editing through technology and on paper. I feel that I am at an advantage in both the writing and editing aspects through these experiences. Sharing real stories and other writings for both personal and business purposes allows one to share from an emotional and professional level. I've been approached to help with memoirs as well as business documents. It is an incredible gift to give your time, effort, and creativity to others to help them put their ideas in writing.

Another outcome is that I have been invited to speak with women at Serenity House on a quarterly basis to talk about self-worth, goals, support systems, and faith. I would love for this to expand to other places and groups.

Name: Lisa Oddo

Business Name: Words of Wisdom Editing & Consulting

Title: Editor/Author/Teacher/Tutor/Commercial Warehouse Owner & Landlord

Contact Email: missoddo@att.net

Volume: *Overcoming Mediocrity Remarkable Women*